SPORTS *in* AMERICA 1950–1959

JIM GIGLIOTTI

SERIES FOREWORD BY LARRY KEITH

Facts On File, Inc.

1950–1959
Sports in America

Facts On File, Inc.
132 West 31st Street
New York NY 10001

Library of Congress Cataloging-in-Publication Data

Sports in America / produced by the Shoreline Publishing Group.
v. cm.
Includes bibliographical references and indexes.
Contents: [1] 1910-1919 / by James Buckley, Jr. and John Walters — [2] 1920-1939 / by John Walters — [3] 1940-1949 / by Phil Barber — [4] 1950-1959 / by Jim Gigliotti — [5] 1960-1969 / by David Fischer — [6] 1970-1979 / by Timothy J. Seeberg and Jim Gigliotti — [7] 1980-1989 / by Michael Teitelbaum — [8] 1990-2003 / by Bob Woods.

ISBN 0-8160-5233-6 (hc : set : alk. paper) — ISBN 0-8160-5234-4 (hc : v. 1 : alk. paper) — ISBN 0-8160-5235-2 (hc : v. 2 : alk. paper) — ISBN 0-8160-5236-0 (hc : v. 3 : alk. paper) — ISBN 0-8160-5237-9 (hc : v. 4 : alk. paper) — ISBN 0-8160-5238-7 (hc : v. 5 : alk. paper) — ISBN 0-8160-5239-5 (hc : v. 6 : alk. paper) — ISBN 0-8160-5240-9 (hc : v. 7 :alk. paper) — ISBN 0-8160-5241-7 (hc : v. 8 : alk. paper)

1. Sports—United States—History. I. Buckley, James, 1963- . II. Shoreline Publishing Group. III. Facts on File, Inc.

GV583.S6826 2004
796'.0973'0904—dc22

2004004276

Facts On File books are available at special discounts when purchased in bulk quantities for businesses, associations, institutions, or sales promotions. Please call our Special Sales Department in New York at (212) 967-8800 or (800) 322-8755.

You can find Facts On File on the World Wide Web at http://www.factsonfile.com

Produced by the Shoreline Publishing Group LLC
President/Editorial Director: James Buckley Jr.
Contributing Editor: Beth Adelman
Text design by Thomas Carling, Carling Design, Inc.
Cover design by Pehrsson Design and Cathy Rincon
Index by Nanette Cardon, IRIS

Photo credits: Page 1: Courtesy Sports Immortals, Inc. This is the actual home plate from the Polo Grounds used in October 1951. It was stepped on by Bobby Thomson after hitting a historic home run for the New York Giants. The plate is signed by Thomson; the photo also shows a 1951 Giants program (see page 23). All interior photos courtesy AP/Wide World except for the following: Corbis: 25, 36, 43, 57, 70; NFL Photos: 62. Sports icons by Bob Eckstein.

Printed in the United States of America.

VH PKG 10 9 8 7 6 5 4 3 2 1

This book is printed on acid-free paper.

CONTENTS

Champion golfer Ben Hogan (page 13)

FOREWORD

BY LARRY KEITH

IN THE FALL OF 1984, STUDENTS AT COLUMBIA University's prestigious Graduate School of Journalism requested that a new course be added to the curriculum—sports journalism.

Sports journalism? In the graduate program of an Ivy League institution? Get serious.

But the students were serious, and, as students will do, they persisted. Eventually, the school formed a committee to interview candidates for the position of "adjunct professor." As it happened, though, the committee wasn't just looking for a professional sports journalist to teach the course part time. That august body wanted to hear clear and convincing arguments that the course should be offered at all.

In other words, did sports matter? And, more to the point, should an institution that administered the Pulitzer Prize, the highest award in journalism, associate itself with the coverage of "fun and games?"

Two decades later, I am pleased to say that Columbia did decide to offer the course and that it remains in the curriculum. With modest pride, I confess that I helped make the arguments that swayed the committee and became the new adjunct professor.

I reflected on that experience when the *Sports in America* editors invited me to write the Foreword to this important series. I said then, and I say now, "Sport is an integral part of American society and requires the attention of a competent and vigilant press." For our purposes here, I might also add, "because it offers insights to our history and culture."

Sports in America is much more than a compilation of names, dates, and facts. Each volume chronicles accomplishments, advances, and expansions of the possible. Not just in the physical ability to run faster, jump higher, or hit a ball farther, but in the cognitive ability to create goals and analyze how to achieve them. In this way, sports, the sweaty offspring of recreation and competition, resemble any other field of endeavor. I certainly wouldn't equate the race for a gold medal with the race to the moon, but the essentials are the same: the application of talent, determination, research, practice, and hard work to a meaningful objective.

Sports matter because they represent the best and worst of us. They give us flesh-and-blood examples of courage and skill. They often embody a heroic human interest story, about overcoming poverty, injustice, injury, or disease. The phrase, "Sports is a microcosm of life," could also be, "Life is a microcosm of sports." Consider racial issues, for example. When Jackie Robinson of the Brooklyn Dodgers broke through Major League Baseball's color barrier in 1947, the significance extended beyond the national pastime. Precisely because baseball *was* the national pastime, this important event reverberated throughout American society.

To be sure, black stars from individual sports had preceded him (notably Joe Louis in boxing and Jesse Owens in track and field), and others would follow (Arthur Ashe in tennis and Tiger Woods in golf), but Robinson stood out as an important member of a *team*. He wasn't just playing with the Dodgers, he was traveling with them, dressing with them, eating with them, living with them. The benefits of integration, the recognition of its humanity, could be appreciated far beyond the borough of Brooklyn.

Sports have always been a laboratory for social issues. Robinson integrated big-league box scores eight years before the U.S. Supreme Court ordered the integration of public schools. Women's official debut in the Olympic Games, though limited to swimming, came in 1912, seven years before they got the right to vote. So even if these sports were late in opening their doors, in another way they were ahead of their time. And if it was necessary to break down some of those doors—Title IX support since 1972 for female college athletics comes to mind—so be it.

Another area of social importance, particularly as it affects young people, is substance abuse. High school, college, and professional teams are united in their opposition to the illegal use of drugs, tobacco, and alcohol. In most venues, testing is mandatory and tolerance is zero. Perhaps the most celebrated case occurred at the 1988 Olympic Games, when Canada's Ben Johnson surrendered his 100-meter gold medal after failing a drug test. Some athletes have lost their careers, and even their lives, to substance abuse. Other athletes have used their fame and success to caution young people about submitting to peer pressure and making poor choices.

Fans care about sports and sports personalities because they provide entertainment and identity. But they aren't the only ones who root, root, root for the home team. Government bodies come on board because sports spur local economies. When a city council votes to help underwrite the cost of a stadium or give financial advantages to the owners of a team, it affects the pocketbook of every taxpayer, not to mention the local ecosystem. When high schools and colleges allocate significant resources to athletics, administrators believe they are serving the greater good, but at what cost? These decisions are relevant far beyond the sports page.

In World War II, America's sporting passion inspired President Franklin Roosevelt to say professional games should not be cancelled. He felt the benefits to the national psyche outweighed the security risk of gathering huge crowds at central locations. In 2001, another generation of fans also continued to attend large-scale sports events because to do otherwise would "let the terrorists win." Being there, yelling your lungs out, cheering victory and bemoaning defeat, is a cleansing, even therapeutic exercise. The security check at the gate is just another price of stepping inside.

Unfortunately, there's a downside to all this. The notion that "Sports build character" is better expressed "Sports *reveal* character." We've witnessed too many coaches and athletes break the rules of fair play and good conduct, on and off the field. We've even seen violence and cheating in youth sports, often by parents of a (supposed) future superstar. We've watched fans "celebrate" championships with destructive behavior. I would argue, however, that these flaws are the exception, not the rule, that the good of sports outweighs the bad, that many of life's success stories took root on an athletic field.

Any serious examination of sports leads, inevitably, to the question of athletes as role models. Pro basketball star Charles Barkley created quite a stir in 1993 when he declared in a Nike shoe commercial, "I am not paid to be a role model." The knee-jerk response was, "But kids look up to you!" Barkley was right to raise the issue, though. He was saying that, in making lifestyle choices in language, clothing, and behavior, young people should look elsewhere for role models—ideally in their own home, to responsible parents.

The fact remains, however, that athletes occupy an exalted place in our society, at least when they are magnified in the mass media, and especially in the big-business, money-motivated sports. The athletes we venerate can be as young as a high school basketball player or as old as a Hall of Famer. (They can even be dead, as Babe Ruth's commercial longevity attests.) They are honored and coddled in a way few mortals are. We are quick—too quick—to excuse their excesses and ignore their indulgences. They influence the way we live (the food on our table, the cars in our driveway) and think (Ted Williams inspired patriotism as a fighter pilot during World War II and the Korean conflict; Muhammad Ali's opposition to the Vietnam War on religious grounds, validated by the Supreme Court, inspired the peace movement). No wonder we elect them—track stars, football coaches, baseball pitchers—to represent us in government. Meanwhile, television networks pay exorbitant sums to sports leagues so their teams can pay fortunes for players' services.

It has always been this way. If we, as a nation, love sports, then we, quite naturally, will love the men and women who play them best. In return, they give us entertainment, release, and inspiration. From the beginning of the 20th century until now, *Sports in America* is their story—and ours.

Larry Keith is a former writer and editor at Sports Illustrated. *He covered baseball and college basketball* and *edited the official Olympic programs in 1996, 2000 and 2002. He is a former adjunct professor of sports journalism at Columbia University and is a member of the Board of Visitors of the University of North Carolina School of Journalism.*

INTRODUCTION 1950–1959

TODAY, PEOPLE LOOK BACK ON THE 1950s with misty-eyed nostalgia. It was the time of the hip-swiveling, ground-breaking music of Elvis Presley, the wacky comedy of *I Love Lucy*, the screaming teens of *American Bandstand*, the fads of 3-D movies, and college kids stuffing themselves into phone booths.

It all seemed so simple and innocent then. Of course, there was that hydrogen bomb thing, too, with the world for the first time facing the possibility that humans could destroy themselves completely. The Cold War, a war of competing ideologies, bred constant tension between the Soviet Union and the West. Hearings led by Senator Joseph McCarthy unsuccessfully sought Communists in every part of the government, in the process ruining hundreds of lives. The Cold War heated up on the Korean Peninsula, and the Korean War blazed from 1950 to 1953. A cheating scandal hit a popular television quiz show. And racial tensions grew, especially in the South.

Indeed, as was the case in any other decade, the 1950s were a mishmash of the good and bad, the wonderful and the tragic, the thrilling and the ordinary. And, as in any other decade, sports in America provided a similar mix of highlights and lowlights.

Among the most noteworthy highlights was the gradual racial integration of the playing fields in the 1950s. Football and baseball had been integrated in the second half of the 1940s, and African-American players dotted rosters in those sports with more frequency and growing acceptance. In 1950, Earl Lloyd, Chuck Cooper, and Nat "Sweetwater" Clifton took to the court in the National Basketball Association (NBA), thus integrating that sport. Althea Gibson became the first African American to play in the U.S. Open tennis tournament. By the mid-1950s, catcher Elston Howard became the first black player on the New York Yankees—one of Major League Baseball's last teams to become integrated.

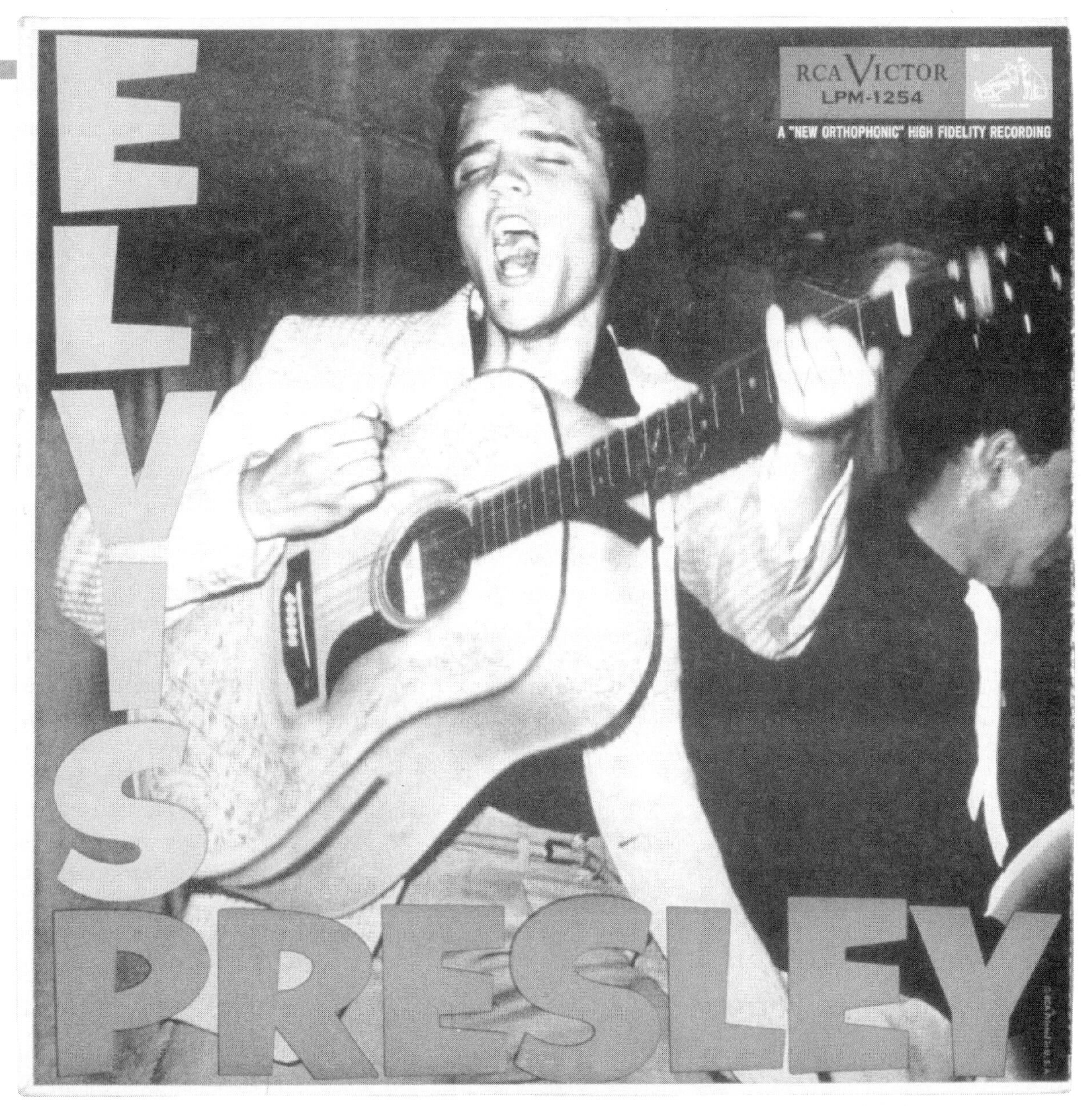

American Idol *Elvis Presley became a national phenomenon in the 1950s with his ground-breaking music.*

Still, it was a sign of the times that the University of San Francisco's unbeaten 1951 football team was not invited to a postseason bowl game because the squad included black players. And that Mississippi State's basketball team in 1959, winners of 24 out of 25 games and ranked number three in the country, declined an invitation to play in the National Collegiate Athletic Association (NCAA) championship because that tournament was integrated.

1950–1959

While some people viewed the world only in terms of black and white, almost everyone began viewing it in black and white—on television. The exciting new medium quickly moved from luxury to necessity in the '50s. And its growing influence on sports could not be overstated. For the first time, images of American sports heroes in action were not just in the fans' imaginations, static newspaper photos, or grainy newsreel footage. Fans could see their favorite stars live on national television.

While all the major sports profited from the increased exposure of television, professional football may have been the biggest beneficiary. The National Football League (NFL) long had taken a back seat to college football in many parts of the country. But when viewers from coast to coast watched the Baltimore Colts win a thrilling, sudden-death overtime game against the New York Giants for the 1958 NFL title (see page 78), a nation was hooked.

Witch Hunt *Senator Joseph McCarthy's (left) crusade against Communism captivated the public in the 1950s—but also led to his eventual disgrace.*

It didn't hurt sports, either, that in the prosperity of post-World War II, men and women had more disposable income. The rapidly expanding consumer culture funneled more money into sports than ever before. Sports soon would be not so much a diversion but an integral part of everyday life. The growing market was such that in 1954, it spawned the birth of *Sports Illustrated.* The cover date of the first magazine was August 16, 1954, and it featured Atlanta Braves slugger Eddie Mathews taking a mighty swing. Cover price: 25 cents. Today, *Sports Illustrated* remains the most widely circulated national sports magazine (though the cover price is no longer 25 cents).

In the major sports, dynasties were the story. The Yankees played in eight World Series in the 1950s, winning six of them. Yankees icon Joe DiMaggio retired following the 1951 season, but a new phenomenon, Mickey Mantle, took over in center field in Yankee Stadium in 1952. Mantle's huge home runs became legendary, and he received the ultimate honor when he was assigned number 6 (he eventually switched to 7)—joining the ranks of single-digit Yankee greats such as Babe Ruth (3), Lou Gehrig (4), and DiMaggio (5).

Even when the Yankees didn't win the World Series, it still was a New York story: From the National League, the New York Giants won in 1954 and the Brooklyn Dodgers in 1955. Fans in the Big Apple had only to board a subway to see every game in the World Series in five different seasons of the '50s.

The Cleveland Browns joined the NFL from the defunct All-American Football Conference in 1950 and made it to the title game the next six years (and seven of eight), winning three. Cleveland's Paul Brown was an innovative head coach who revolutionized the game with full-time coaching staffs, radio communication with his quarterback, extensive college scouting, and much more.

In basketball, the Minneapolis Lakers won four of five NBA championships to start the decade, then made another finals appearance in 1959, when the torch was passed to the Boston Celtics. Lakers center George Mikan was pro basketball's first formidable big man, and had a profound impact on the sport.

In the National Hockey League (NHL), the dominant team was north of the border. The Montreal Canadiens closed the 1950s with four consecutive Stanley Cup championships.

By the end of the 1950s, change was in the air. In sports, baseball's Dodgers and Giants had left New York for the promise of new stadiums and new fans on the West Coast. The Lakers' and Browns' dynasties would give way to those of the Celtics and Packers. The new American Football League (1960) was about to challenge the NFL's stranglehold on professional football.

Yes, the 1960s would bring sweeping changes to sports and society. That decade can wait, though.

Black and White and Pinstripes *Nearly a decade after Jackie Robinson broke baseball's color barrier with the Brooklyn Dodgers, Elston Howard integrated the New York Yankees.*

Maybe it wasn't all Elvis and phone booth stuffing in the 1950s. Let us look back at the world of sports at a time when America was still moving slowly toward change.

1950

The Bears Are Almost Perfect

For the second consecutive year, the University of California's football team forged a 10–0 regular-season record and swept to the Pacific Coast Conference championship. And for the second consecutive year, the California Golden Bears lost in the Rose Bowl.

In the previous season, California was ranked fourth in the nation when number-seven Northwestern University pulled an upset on New Year's Day, 1949. This time, the Golden Bears were third in the nation, behind only the University of Notre Dame and University of Oklahoma, when sixth-ranked Ohio State spoiled their perfect season with a 17–14 victory on January 2, 1950.

With the game tied at 14–14 late in the fourth quarter, an errant punt snap helped position the Ohio State Buckeyes on California's 13-yard line. Three plays later, Ohio State's Jimmy Hague kicked the game-winning field goal from 17 yards with less than two minutes left. Buckeyes fullback Fred Morrison ran for 127 yards and was named the player of the game. The game drew a record 100,983 fans.

Twice as Nice for CCNY

City College of New York (CCNY) pulled off an unprecedented double by winning college basketball's National Invitational Tournament (NIT) and NCAA tournaments in the same season. What's more, the CCNY Beavers were unranked heading into the tournament season in March.

CCNY had a young squad with four sophomores in its starting lineup. After going 17–5 in the regular season, the Beavers reeled off a string of unlikely upsets over some of college basketball's top powerhouses. First, there was a 19-point victory over the defending-champion University of San Francisco to open the NIT. Then a shocking, 39-point rout of third-ranked University of Kentucky in the quarterfinals. It was the worst loss in the history of Kentucky basketball. After a 62–52 victory over Duquesne University in the semifinals, the Beavers upset number-one Bradley University in the NIT final, 69–61.

In the eight-team NCAA tournament, CCNY won the Eastern Regional by edging number-two Ohio State by one point and number-five North Carolina State by five points, setting up a rematch with Bradley.

Open Season *Ben Hogan's victory in the U.S. Open (page 13) capped his remarkable comeback from injury.*

The Beavers' 11-point second-half lead dwindled to one point in the closing seconds, but they held on to win 71–68.

Forward Irwin Dambrot, the lone senior in CCNY's starting lineup, scored 15 points in the final and was named the tournament's most outstanding player.

Red Wings Work Overtime

On April 23, the Detroit Red Wings won hockey's Stanley Cup in dramatic fashion, beating the New York Rangers 4–3 with a goal in overtime in game seven. It was the first time the NHL

The Lake Show *The Minneapolis Lakers, led by center George Mikan (shooting), had the dominant team in the fledgling days of the National Basketball Association.*

championship had been won with an overtime goal in a winner-take-all game.

The Red Wings were heavy favorites after winning the six-team NHL's regular-season title, while the Rangers squeaked into the playoffs with fewer wins than losses and a fourth-place finish. But New York upset the second-place Montreal Canadiens in the semifinals, while the Red Wings eliminated the third-place Toronto Maple Leafs.

In the finals, the Rangers were on the verge of a surprising championship after taking a three-games-to-two lead, then jumping to a 2–0 lead in game six. Detroit battled back to win that game 5–4, however, and force a game seven.

In the final game, New York again scored twice to jump out in front, but the Red Wings tied it at 3–3 at the end of the regulation three periods. After one scoreless overtime, Detroit's Pete Babando scored the winning goal at 8:31 of the second overtime period.

Great Lakes

The Minneapolis Lakers became the first champions of the newly formed National Basketball Association (NBA) when they won the league finals in six games over the Syracuse Nationals on April 23.

Big center George Mikan (see the box on page 13) was the dominant force for the Lakers, who went 51–17 and tied the Rochester Royals for the Central Division title in the regular season. Mikan averaged a league-best 27.4 points per game during the regular season, then topped that in the playoffs by averaging a whopping 31.3 points per game. He scored 40 points in a 110–95 victory over Syracuse in the clinching game of the finals.

The 17-team NBA was born out of a merger between a pair of leagues started in the 1940s—the National Basketball League and the Basketball Association of America.

Hogan's Comeback

It all happened so fast that Ben Hogan (1912–1997) had little time to react. When he was a few hours outside of El Paso, Texas, a bus traveling in the opposite direction on a two-lane highway pulled out of its lane to pass a slow-moving car. The bus plowed head-on into Hogan's car.

The golfing great threw himself in front of his wife to protect her, and she suffered only minor injuries. Hogan was not so fortunate, however. He had severe injuries in the near-fatal crash, including a broken collarbone, ankle, and rib, and two fractures of his pelvis. Doctors said he might never walk again—let alone play golf.

That was in February 1949. Fast forward to June 1950. Hogan not only defied doctors' expectations and returned to the golf course, he also returned to the form that helped him lead the Professional Golfers' Association (PGA) Tour in money won three times during the 1940s.

George Mikan: The First Big Man

Few athletes have had as profound an impact on any sport as George Mikan (b.1924) had on basketball. At 6-feet-10½, Mikan ushered in the era of the big man in basketball. His deft shooting touch and remarkable quickness hadn't been seen in a man his size, and enabled him to thoroughly dominate opponents from his center position.

While he was with the Minneapolis Lakers from 1947 to 1954, Mikan became a drawing card the likes of which professional basketball had never seen. In nine professional seasons, Mikan led his teams to seven league championships. He averaged 23.1 points per game in his career and led the league in scoring three times. He led the league in rebounding twice, although that statistic was not officially kept until the later stages of his career. He played in each of the NBA's first four all-star games.

Statistics don't tell the whole story, though. Mikan changed the game, first in college at DePaul University, then in the pros. In college, Mikan stood underneath the basket and swatted opposing shots away. As a result, the goaltending rule was instituted making it illegal to block a shot once it is on the way down toward the basket. In the pros, the lane, or area in front of the basket, was widened from six feet to 12 feet because of him. (Offensive players cannot remain in the lane for more than three consecutive seconds; the wider lane was to try to keep Mikan farther away from the basket.)

In 1954, when he was only 30 years old, Mikan surprised the Lakers by announcing his retirement. He wanted to spend more time with his growing family. He came back briefly in the 1955-56 season, then retired for good.

Later, he became commissioner of the rival American Basketball Association in the 1960s, and was the man responsible for that league's famous red, white, and blue basketballs.

In 1950, the Associated Press named Mikan the greatest basketball player of the first half-century.

1950

And on the second nine holes (called the "back nine") of the U.S. Open at the Merion Golf Club in Ardmore, Pennsylvania, Hogan had a three-stroke lead with six holes to play. The rugged final-day format, however—golfers played 36 holes on Saturday—proved to be too much for Hogan, who still was recuperating from his injuries. He staggered home on aching legs and finished in a three-way tie with George Fazio and Lloyd Mangrum.

The tie set up an 18-hole playoff the next day. The only question was whether Hogan's legs would hold up, because his will was indomitable and his ball-striking was unparalleled.

Hogan not only held up, but he got better as the round went on. After shooting 36 on the front nine, he finished the back nine in 33 strokes. His score of 69 gave him a relatively easy victory. He beat Mangrum by four strokes and Fazio by six to cap one of the most remarkable comebacks in the history of sports.

World Class Wins

The United States' stunning upset of England in the 1950 World Cup was the third of only six wins ever for the Americans in the world's premier soccer tournament. The list of victories:

1930	United States 3, Belgium 0 (Group play)
1930	United States 3, Paraguay 0 (Group play)
1950	United States 1, England 0 (Group play)
1994	United States 2, Colombia 1 (Group play)
2002	United States 3, Portugal 2 (Group play)
2002	United States 2, Mexico 0 (Round of 16)

A Stunning Upset for the United States

Uruguay surprised host Brazil 2–1 before 174,000 fans to win soccer's World Cup in 1950. Uruguay's win wasn't the biggest upset of the tournament, though. That distinction belonged to the United States, which stunned England—and just about everyone else—with a 1–0 win in an early-round game on June 29.

England was generally considered the best soccer team in the world, and because of World War II there had not been a World Cup since 1938 to disprove that notion. English and American players alike expected a one-sided game, with at least one American player even quoted in later years that a "three- or four-goal loss would have been respectable."

Instead, Joe Gaetjens headed in a goal in the first half to give the Americans a 1–0 lead. The one goal held up when the English squad narrowly missed on numerous scoring attempts in the second half.

The biggest upset in World Cup history was met with disbelief in England. The English had been such overwhelming favorites that when the score came over the news wires, some newspaper editors assumed there must have been a mistake. Instead of United States 1, England 0, they figured it must have been United States 1, England 10!

A Taxing Loss for Louis

Almost two years after his last boxing match, Joe Louis (1914–1981) came out of retirement to fight heavyweight-champion Ezzard Charles (1921–1975) at Yankee Stadium in New York on September 27. Boxing fans were saddened to see that the legendary 36-year-old was a shadow of his former self.

Louis, who had retired still owning the heavyweight title he first earned in 1937, was trying to become the first man ever to regain the crown. The return of the popular "Brown Bomber," though, was spurred less by his quest for history than a need to raise enough money to pay back taxes to the Internal Revenue Service.

Charles had little trouble dispatching the former champ. Although he never knocked Louis to the mat, he pummeled him with a barrage of punches that Louis could do little to counter. The 15-round decision was unanimous, and Charles retained the heavyweight title he gained after Louis "retired" in 1949. Louis' loss was only the second of his career, and his first since 1936.

Though clearly not the boxer he once was, Louis fought often over the next year. He won eight non-title fights before he was knocked out in the eighth round by Rocky Marciano (1923–1969) on October 26, 1951. After that, his retirement was final.

New York Story

The New York Yankees, New York Giants, and Brooklyn Dodgers were Major League Baseball's dominant teams in the 1950s. The decade's World Series champions:

1950	New York Yankees
1951	New York Yankees
1952	New York Yankees
1953	New York Yankees
1954	New York Giants
1955	Brooklyn Dodgers
1956	New York Yankees
1957	Milwaukee Braves
1958	New York Yankees
1959	Los Angeles Dodgers

The Yankees' Annual Fall Ritual

In what had become almost an annual fall ritual, the New York Yankees were baseball's champions again. Their four-game sweep of the Philadelphia Phillies in the World Series in October gave them their second straight title and their ninth baseball championship in 15 seasons.

The Phillies were baseball's "Whiz Kids." They clinched the N.L. pennant on the last day of the season, when Dick Sisler (b.1920) hit a three-run home run in the top of the 10th inning to beat the Brooklyn Dodgers 4–1 in Brooklyn The Dodgers, who needed a victory to force a playoff, had the potential winning run thrown out at the plate by Phillies centerfielder Richie Ashburn (1927–1997) in the bottom of the ninth inning.

Yankees' pitchers shackled Philadelphia's hitters in the World Series, though. Vic Raschi (1919–1988) pitched a two-hit shutout in the opening game to set the tone. The Phillies batted only .203 and managed only five runs, with no home runs, in the Series.

1950

The Yankees won three more World Series to make it five straight titles before their streak finally ended in 1954.

Debut Hit

The Cleveland Browns dominated play for four years in the All-America Football Conference (AAFC), but most football experts assumed they'd get their comeuppance when they joined the NFL in 1950. Not so. The Browns proved they belonged from their very first game.

Cleveland won all four AAFC titles and went 47–4–3 from 1946 to 1949 before the league folded. The Browns, San Francisco 49ers, and Baltimore Colts were incorporated into the NFL in time for the 1950 season. And to start things off, NFL Commissioner Bert Bell (1895–1959) pitted Cleveland against the defending-champion Philadelphia Eagles at Philadelphia's Municipal Stadium. The Browns were ready. "Four years of ridicule helped us get ready," Cleveland head coach Paul Brown (1908–1991) said.

The NFL long had looked down on AAFC teams. In fact, when the AAFC was first formed, NFL Commissioner Elmer Layden reportedly said, "Tell them to get a ball first." That wasn't exactly what he really said, but the implication was clear: The NFL wasn't worried about a startup league. "They would say that their worst team could beat our best team," Browns quarterback Otto Graham (b.1921) said. "We read that kind of stuff for four years."

Everyone who thought the September 16 game between Philadelphia and Cleveland would be a mismatch was right. But it was the Browns who had no trouble. Graham passed for 346 yards and three touchdowns and ran for another score in a 35–10 victory.

Cleveland went on to win 10 of 12 regular-season games, losing only a pair of close contests to the New York Giants. The Browns avenged those defeats, however, with an 8–3 victory over New York in a conference playoff game. That left the NFL in the uncomfortable position of having one of the former AAFC teams playing for the championship in their first year in the league. "No one wanted an outsider winning the league championship," Browns tackle and kicker Lou Groza (1924–2000) said.

"The NFL didn't like us," receiver Dante Lavelli (b.1923) said. But like it or not, the Browns were for real. They were loaded, with future Pro Football Hall of Famers such as Graham, Groza, Lavelli, fullback Marion Motley (1920–1999), and defensive end Len Ford (1926–1972).

A tense, exciting championship game in Cleveland against the Los Angeles Rams on December 24 came down to the wire. Graham passed for four touchdowns, but a missed extra point left the Browns trailing 28–27 in the final period.

Graham lost a fumble midway through the fourth quarter, but, with 1:50 left, Cleveland had one last chance beginning from its 32-yard line. Graham scrambled for 14 yards, then completed passes of 15, 16, and 12 yards to move the ball to the Rams' 11-yard line. After Graham gained three yards on a short run up the middle, Groza came on to kick the winning field goal from 16 yards with 20 seconds remaining. The Browns won 30–28 and were NFL champions.

Other Milestones of 1950

✔ In its fourth year, the College World Series moved to Omaha, Nebraska, where it found a permanent home. The University of Texas was the first champion in the new venue.

✔ On August 8, American Florence Chadwick swam the English Channel, a distance of 20 miles, in a record time of 13 hours and 23 minutes.

✔ Tennis star Louise Brough won a rare triple at Wimbledon in July: She captured titles in singles, doubles, and mixed doubles in 1950.

Florence Chadwick

✔ Margaret Osborne-du Pont won the U.S. Open women's singles tennis title in September, for the third consecutive year.

✔ In college football, Purdue University beat top-ranked Notre Dame 28–14 on October 7. It was the first loss in 40 games for defending national champions Notre Dame.

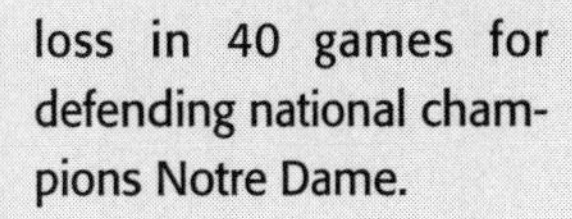

✔ The Los Angeles Rams became the first pro football team to have an insignia on their helmets. The team hand-painted yellow ram's horns on their blue leather helmets.

Professional Basketball Is Integrated

Professional football had been integrated in 1946. Jackie Robinson (1919–1972) made his big-league debut in baseball in 1947. Finally, professional basketball eliminated its color barrier in 1950, when a trio of players joined the NBA.

First, the Boston Celtics selected forward Chuck Cooper (1926–1984) in the second round of the NBA draft in 1950, making him the first African-American player to be drafted by an NBA team. The same year, forward Nat "Sweetwater" Clifton (1927–1990) became the first African-American player to sign with an NBA team when the New York Knicks signed the former Harlem Globetrotters star to a contract. Then, on October 31, forward Earl "Big Cat" Lloyd (b.1928) became the first African-American player to take the court when he made his debut for the Washington Capitols in a game against the Rochester Royals.

Lloyd played in just seven games that year, but went on to play six years for the Syracuse Nationals and two for the Detroit Pistons. He had his best season in 1954–55, when he averaged 10.2 points and 7.7 rebounds while helping the Nationals to the NBA title.

Cooper averaged 6.7 points per game in six NBA seasons, including a career-best 9.9 points for the Celtics in his rookie year.

Clifton averaged 10 points and 8.2 rebounds in eight seasons. He averaged a career-best 13.1 points in 1954–55 and played in the All-Star Game in 1957.

1951

Bowl Day

The new year began with an old story: For the third year in a row, the University of California took an undefeated team to play in the Rose Bowl on January 1 . . . and, for the third year in a row, lost.

The Golden Bears were 9–0–1 heading into the Rose Bowl and were ranked number four in the nation. The University of Michigan Wolverines managed only a 5–3–1 record during the regular season. But fullback Don Dufek rushed for a pair of touchdowns in the fourth quarter to lift the Wolverines to a 14–6 upset. Dufek ran for 113 yards and was named the game's most valuable player.

Before the game, future President Dwight D. Eisenhower was slated to be the Rose Parade's grand marshal. But when the Korean War broke out, the general was ordered back to military service by President Harry Truman. Eisenhower sent an injured private, Robert Gray, to represent the troops in Korea as the parade's grand marshal.

California wasn't the only team to falter on New Year's day. It wasn't even the biggest to fall, in fact. National-champion University of Oklahoma was upset by an inspired University of Kentucky team in the Sugar Bowl.

The national champion was crowned in those days before the bowl games, which really were a reward for a successful season. Oklahoma won 10 games without a loss in 1950 and stretched its unbeaten string to 31 games. On January 1, however, 10–1 Kentucky beat the Oklahoma Sooners 13–7. The Kentucky Wildcats' Wilbur Jamerson scored both his team's touchdowns, one on a 25-yard catch and the other on a one-yard run.

Kentucky's head coach was Paul "Bear" Bryant (1913–1983), who would go on to considerable fame as the head coach at the University of Alabama.

St. Valentine's Day Massacre

For the sixth and last time in their career, boxing greats Sugar Ray Robinson (1921–1989) and Jake LaMotta (b.1921) stepped into the ring against one another. LaMotta was defending his middleweight crown against Robinson, who held the welterweight title. Although Robinson won four of the previous five

Hugs All Around *Bobby Thomson is the center of attention after hitting the "Shot Heard 'Round the World" (page 23).*

fights between the two, some of the bouts were among the toughest of his career. LaMotta's lone victory came in 1943 and was Robinson's first loss in 41 career fights.

At Chicago Stadium, LaMotta hung tough in the early rounds, even taking the offensive at times. But the bout quickly turned. Robinson was too athletic and too strong for his opponent. First, he wore down LaMotta, then he started pummeling him. In the 13th round, the fight was stopped. Robinson won the title.

Because LaMotta took such a brutal beating and because the date of the fight was February 14, the match has gone

1951

down in boxing history as the "St. Valentine's Day Massacre."

Hoops Scandal

The biggest news off the playing fields in 1951 involved a college basketball scandal that rocked sports fans around the country. In mid-February, three players from City College of New York were arrested for fixing games. That is, they purposely did not try their best so that games would turn out favorably for certain gamblers.

The news was shocking. CCNY had been one of the feel-good stories of 1950 after winning both the NIT and NCAA tournaments in the same season (see page 10). But that wasn't even the worst part. At first, most people believed the scandal was limited to games played at New York's Madison Square Garden. That turned out to be just the start, though. Eventually, the scandal spread to cities from coast to coast and was a major black eye for college sports.

All-Star Idea

With basketball reeling from its college scandal, NBA publicist Haskell Cohen had an idea to win back fans: an annual midseason All-Star Game.

Cohen's idea had its skeptics, but it proved to be a smash. More than 10,000 fans watched at the Boston Garden on March 2 as the East beat the West, 111–94, in the NBA's first All-Star Game. "Easy" Ed Macauley of the hometown Celtics was the game's most valuable player, after scoring 20 points.

The NBA All-Star Game has been scheduled every year since.

Centers of Attention

Two centerfielders who were destined to rank among the greatest players in baseball history broke into the major leagues in New York during the spring of 1951. Both players eventually became members of the Baseball Hall of Fame.

In the Bronx, Mickey Mantle (1931–1995) joined the Yankees. He batted a modest .267 with 13 home runs in 341 at-bats. Mantle went on to hit .298 with 536 home runs in his 18-year career.

At the Polo Grounds in Manhattan, heralded rookie Willie Mays (b.1931) started slowly for the Giants, but then came on strong to bat .274 with 20 home runs. He played 22 seasons in his career and hit

Golf Summit

As memorable as Ben Hogan's victory was at the 1951 U.S. Open (see page 21), perhaps the most significant development in golf that year occurred off the course.

In the spring of 1951, representatives of the Royal and Ancient Golf Club of St. Andrews, the United States Golf Association, the Australian Golf Union, and the Royal Canadian Golf Association convened in Scotland and England. Their mission: to find common ground among increasingly disparate rules.

By the end of the meeting, they had agreed to a uniform code of rules. This had a significant impact on the growing popularity of golf around the world.

Little Ball *Pinch hitter Eddie Gaedel was a pint-sized promotional stunt of St. Louis Browns owner Bill Veeck.*

.302 while slugging 660 home runs. Only Hank Aaron (b.1935) with 755, and Babe Ruth (1895–1948) with 714, ever hit more home runs.

Mays also is the answer to a trivia question. He was the man on deck waiting to bat when Bobby Thomson (b.1923) hit his famous home run in the pennant-winning playoff game against the Dodgers (see page 23).

Hogan Tames the Monster

Ben Hogan won his second consecutive U.S. Open golf tournament June 16.

Hogan shot a final-round 67 at the rugged Oakland Hills Country Club in Birmingham, Michigan. That Hogan shot a 67 is not news. He was one of the greatest golfers ever, and he also won the Masters in 1951. But the average score for the final round of the Open was 75, and only two players shot rounds under par at Oakland Hills. The course was so tough that it was dubbed "the Monster."

Hogan called his final round in the 1951 Open the greatest he ever played. Afterward, he reveled that he "brought this course, this monster, to its knees."

Jersey Joe's Revenge

Jersey Joe Walcott knocked out champion Ezzard Charles in the seventh round at Pittsburgh July 18 to

Maureen Connolly:
Tennis' Little Mo

A 5-foot-4, 120-pound teenager took the tennis world by storm in 1951. Maureen Connolly (1934–1969) ascended to the top of the American rankings and became the youngest winner of the prestigious United States Open. Connolly was just 16 years and 11 months when she beat Shirley Fry in three sets to win the U.S. Open. It was the first of three consecutive national titles for Connolly.

For the next three years, "Little Mo" was the top women's tennis player in the world. She forged a remarkable record in tennis' most important events, and in 1953 became the first woman to win the Grand Slam. In tennis, the Slam is made up today of the "major" tournaments: U.S., French, and Australian Opens and Wimbledon. In Connolly's day, the first three were not called "Opens," and in fact were for amateur players only, but were still considered to be the top events. In her most dominant stretch, she won nine consecutive majors she entered, winning 50 matches without a loss.

Sadly, Connolly's playing career came to a sudden end when she severely injured her leg while horseback riding in 1954. She remained active in the game as a tennis instructor, but died of cancer at age 34.

By the way, Little Mo didn't get her nickname because of her size. Instead, it was a tribute to her powerful ground strokes. "Big Mo" at the time was the nickname of the powerful battleship, *U.S.S. Missouri*.

become boxing's new heavyweight champ.

Two years earlier, Charles had beaten Walcott on points to win the title vacated by Joe Louis, who had retired. Charles successfully defended his crown eight times, including once against Walcott, before losing the bout in 1951. Walcott, who was 37 at the time, proved it was no fluke, however, by beating Charles again in 1952.

Small Stunt

Imagine the surprise of the visiting Detroit Tigers when Eddie Gaedel was announced as a pinch-hitter to lead off the second game of a baseball doubleheader in St. Louis against the Browns on August 19. An unknown pinch hitter in the first inning wasn't the surprise, though. The surprise was that Gaedel was a midget!

It was part of a publicity stunt by new Browns owner Bill Veeck (1914–1986), who was trying to drum up interest in the moribund franchise. Gaedel had legitimately been signed to a contract, however, and was allowed to hit. So, wearing number 1/8, he stepped into the batter's box. With his 3-foot-7 frame in a crouch, Gaedel's strike zone was miniscule. Under strict orders not to swing, he looked at four consecutive balls and walked to first base, tipping his hat to the crowd along the way. He was replaced by a pinch runner.

Fans and players, including Tigers pitcher Bob Cain, were laughing. But American League President Will Harridge was not amused. He voided Gaedel's contract the next day, saying it was not in the best interests of baseball. To this day, though, you can still find Gaedel's name in the *Baseball Encyclopedia* . . . with a perfect career on-base percentage of 1.000.

A Good Start

Los Angeles Rams quarterback Norm Van Brocklin (1926–1983), ended the 1951 NFL season by throwing the winning touchdown pass to Tom Fears (1923–2000) in the championship game on December 23. He started it with a record-setting performance in the Rams' opening-game rout of football's New York Yankees.

Van Brocklin shared time at quarterback with Bob Waterfield (1920–1983) for most of the 1950 season. He played the whole game against the Yankees on September 28, though, because Waterfield injured his knee in a preseason game. Van Brocklin made the most of his chance, completing 27 of 41 passes for 554 yards and five touchdowns as the Rams won 54–14. More than 50 years later, his yardage total is still the NFL record.

"It was the finest exhibition of passing I've ever seen," Yankees coach Jimmy Phelan said.

The Shot Heard 'Round the World

The biggest headline of 1951 came from one mighty swing of Bobby Thomson's bat at the Polo Grounds in New York. It came on October 3, in the ninth inning of the third and final game of a National League playoff between Thomson's New York Giants and the Brooklyn Dodgers. When Dodgers pitcher Ralph Branca (b.1926) was summoned from the bullpen to face Thomson, Giants manager Leo Durocher (1905–1991) sidled up to his power-hitting third baseman. "Bobby," Durocher reportedly told Thomson, "if you've ever hit one, hit one now."

Thomson stepped in to face Branca. The Giants trailed 4–2, with one out and runners on second and third. Thomson worked the count to one ball and one strike. Branca wound up and delivered. "There's a long drive," radio broadcaster Russ Hodges (1911–1971) screamed into the microphone. "It's gonna be, I believe . . . The Giants win the pennant! The Giants win the pennant! The Giants win the pennant, and they're going crazy! The Giants win the pennant!"

Thomson's drive cleared the high wall in left field at the Polo Grounds as the Dodgers' Andy Pafko looked up helplessly near the 315-foot sign. When Thomson finished dancing around the bases in unbridled glee, he was mobbed by teammates and thousands of fans who stormed the field. It is one of the most memorable moments in the history of baseball.

As remarkable as Thomson's home run was, it never could have occurred if not for an equally remarkable stretch run by the Giants. In the middle of August, they trailed the Dodgers by a whopping 13 1/2 games. "The Giants is dead," Dodgers manager Charlie Dressen (1898–1966) declared.

The sleeping Giants weren't dead, however, and they awoke to win 37 of their last 44 games. When New York won five games in a row late in the season and Brooklyn lost to Philadelphia 4–3 on

1951

September 28, the frontrunners were tied with two games left. Each team won the next day, and the Giants won again the day after that, then boarded a train bound for New York not knowing the outcome of the Dodgers' game. When the train stopped at a station along the route, the news came: Brooklyn rallied to win 9–8, forcing a three-game playoff.

Thomson homered to help the Giants win the first playoff game, but the Dodgers won the second game in a rout. It looked like Brooklyn was headed to the World Series with a 4–1 lead in the ninth inning of game three with ace Don Newcombe (b.1926) on the mound. But Alvin Dark led off the inning with a single and Don Mueller followed with another single. With one out, Whitey Lockman doubled in a run. Dressen then summoned Branca. The rest, as they say, is history.

The Magic Runs Out

Bobby Thomson's pennant-winning home run for the Giants provided the most memorable highlight of the baseball season in 1951. But it was the New York Yankees who won the World Series in October . . . again.

The Giants won two of the first three games of the Series before the Yankees rallied to win the next three games. It was the third consecutive title for the Bronx Bombers.

Yankees pitcher Ed Lopat pitched all nine innings to win games two and five, allowing only 10 hits and one earned run in 18 innings. In game six, Hank Bauer tripled with the bases loaded to drive in three runs and give the Yankees a 4–1 lead entering the ninth inning—the same score by which the Giants trailed the Dodgers while facing elimination in the playoffs. The Giants loaded the bases with none out and pushed across two runs to pull within 4–3. There would be no dramatic comeback this time, however. Pinch hitter Sal Yvars lined out to end the game, and the Yankees were the champions.

Brown Out

For the first time in the six-year history of their team, the Cleveland Browns were not a championship football team in 1951.

In 1946, the Browns were charter members of the All-America Football Conference, a league established to rival the NFL. The AAFC folded four years later, however, in large part because Cleveland was so enormously successful that there was little suspense to capture the fans' interest in other cities. The Browns won the AAFC championship all four years of that league's existence.

In 1950, Cleveland joined the NFL. Although the Browns did lose a couple of times along the way, they won the NFL title, too, in their first season in that league (see page 16). It looked like it would be more of the same the next year, when Cleveland bounced back from an opening-game loss to the San Francisco 49ers to win 11 consecutive games heading into the 1951 NFL championship game on December 23 against the Los Angeles Rams.

The Browns beat Los Angeles in the 1950 title game with a last-minute field goal. This time, though, it was the Rams

Other Milestones of 1951

✔ The NFL Pro Bowl game returned after a nine-year absence. In January the American Conference all-stars defeated the National Conference all-stars 28–27.

✔ In the longest game in NBA history on January 6, Indianapolis beat Rochester 75–73. The game went to six overtime periods before producing a winner.

Dub Jones

✔ The University of Kentucky beat Kansas State in the final game on March 27 to win the NCAA basketball title for the third time in four years.

✔ The Rochester Royals beat the New York Knicks in seven games to win the NBA title. Rochester won the first three games of the series, then lost the next three before edging New York 79–75 in the final on April 21.

✔ Toronto beat Montreal in the Stanley Cup Finals in April. Each of the five games in the series went into overtime.

✔ The Cleveland Browns' Dub Jones scored six touchdowns in a 42–21 victory over the Chicago Bears on November 25. Only the Chicago Cardinals Ernie Nevers (in 1929) and the Bears' Gale Sayers (1965) have also scored six touchdowns in an NFL game.

✔ The University of Tennessee won its first national championship in college football.

who made the key play in the fourth quarter. With the score tied at 17–17 midway through the fourth quarter, Rams quarterback Norm Van Brocklin found end Tom Fears between two defenders deep down the field. Van Brocklin's pass hit Fears perfectly in stride, and the end sprinted to complete a 73-yard touchdown. "That was the best thrown pass I ever caught in my life," Fears said after the game.

The Rams won 24–17. They did not win another NFL title until Super Bowl XXXIV following the 1999 season, when the franchise was in St. Louis. Coincidentally, it was another 73-yard touchdown pass—Kurt Warner to Isaac Bruce—that broke a tie game in the fourth quarter and lifted the Rams past the Tennessee Titans.

In Living Color

Television was still a relative luxury to most Americans, but the medium was beginning to assimilate itself more and more into everyday life. In 1950, consumers purchased a record 7 million TV sets. And in 1951, technology took a dramatic step when color television was introduced.

Another major step in 1951: When the Rams beat the Browns for the NFL championship, fans all across the country could watch. The DuMont Network made it the first game ever televised from coast to coast.

The marriage between television and sports was still in the newlywed stage. It proved to be a long and profitable union.

1952

Sugar Bowl Gives Tennessee a Sour Taste

The University of Tennessee may have won college football's national championship in 1951, but the new year got off to a bad start for the Volunteers when they were upset by third-ranked University of Maryland 28–13 in the Sugar Bowl on January 1. It was the second straight year the national champion was beaten in a bowl game, but it would still be more than a decade before the final polls were not taken until after the bowl season.

Maryland fullback Ed Modzelewski was named the game's most valuable player after rushing for 153 yards to help the Terrapins end Tennessee's 20-game winning streak. Maryland's victory was the 12th in its own winning streak, which reached 19 games the next season.

Trailblazers

Pro football, Major League Baseball, and pro basketball had eliminated their color barriers in the late 1940s and early 1950s, but not all the playing fields were level by 1952. The PGA Tour, for instance, still had a rule on the books that tournament golfers had to be Caucasian. In January, popular African-American boxer Joe Louis, an amateur golfer, entered the San Diego Open. When tournament officials balked, the PGA agreed to modify the rule and Louis was allowed to play. It wasn't until 1961, however, that the "Caucasian Clause" was officially removed from the PGA Constitution.

Jackie Robinson (1919–1972), who broke baseball's color barrier with the Brooklyn Dodgers, broke another barrier when he was hired as the director of community activities by NBC in New York. Robinson became the first African-American executive of a major television network.

Something Old, Something New in the NBA

Changes were apparent in the NBA in 1952. The lane was widened from 6 feet to 12 feet for the 1951–52 season, and more and more players were using the revolutionary jump shot. Before this season, most players shot with both feet on the floor—the set shot. Philadelphia 76ers forward Paul Arizin was among a few players who developed the jump shot,

Flying Ace *Hitting a baseball or flying a Marine jet, Ted Williams (page 28) was about the best there ever was.*

that is, jumping off the floor and releasing the ball at the top of the jump, avoiding defenders. Arizin was so effective with his jumper that he usurped dominant center George Mikan as the league's leading scorer, averaging 25.4 points per game.

But the more things changed, the more they stayed the same. Mikan's Minneapolis Lakers were the league's premier team again, and won the title in April for the third time in four years. The streak reached six championships in seven seasons before the run ended.

Still, Minneapolis' 1952 crown did not come easily. The Lakers finished one game behind the defending-champion Rochester Royals in the Western Division before dispatching the Royals three games to one in the conference playoffs.

Minneapolis was heavily favored in the finals over the New York Knickerbockers, who finished third in the Eastern

1952

Division during the regular season but upset the Boston Celtics and Syracuse Nationals in the conference playoffs. After a series of close games that included two overtime thrillers, the series moved to Minneapolis for a decisive game seven. This one wasn't as close. With Mikan pouring in 22 points, the Lakers beat New York, 82–65.

Winter Olympics

Host Norway dominated much of the Winter Olympic Games in February in Oslo, but the United States turned in a strong performance behind figure skater Dick Button (b.1929), speed skater Ken Henry, and skier Andrea Mead Lawrence.

Button successfully defended his 1948 gold medal with a surprise triple loop jump (the first in Olympic competition) that earned him first place on all the judges' cards in Oslo. Henry won the gold in the 500-meter race, while American teammate Don McDermott grabbed the silver. The 19-year-old Lawrence won gold medals in both the regular and giant slalom. The U.S. hockey team also fared well, tying gold medalist Canada in the final game to earn the silver medal.

In the summer, Button cashed in on his skating success by signing a contract to appear in the Ice Capades of 1953. The contract was for a reported $150,000.

Medal Leaders: Winter Olympics

	GOLD	SILVER	BRONZE	TOTAL
Norway	7	3	6	16
USA	4	6	1	11
Finland	3	4	2	9
Austria	2	4	2	8
Germany	3	2	2	7

An American Hero

In 1950, troops from North Korea invaded South Korea and, just five years after the end of World War II, the Korean War had begun. In 1952, the war nearly took the life of Ted Williams (1918–2002), one of America's legendary baseball players.

The "Splendid Splinter," who won six batting titles and hit an amazing .344 in his 19-year baseball career, was called up from the reserves in May, along with major leaguers such as Jerry Coleman and Lloyd Merriman. Williams was a pilot in the U.S. Army during World War II, serving with distinction. Before the Korean War ended in 1953, Williams flew 39 combat missions as a Marine pilot. His plane was hit by enemy fire several times, including once when he had to land his flaming F-9 Panther jet on its belly. He executed the dangerous maneuver and walked away without serious injury, just moments before the plane exploded.

By all accounts, Williams was nearly as great a pilot as he was a hitter. In fact, if not for baseball, his first love, Williams may have had a full-time career as a Marine pilot. "I liked flying," Williams said. "It was the second-best thing that ever happened to me."

Boys Only

The All-American Girls Professional Baseball League was in its tenth season in 1952 (see page 32), but a woman also briefly joined a men's minor league team. The Class B Harrisburg (Pennsylvania) Senators signed Eleanor Engle, a 24-year-old stenographer, to a baseball contract in June.

"She can hit a lot better than some of the fellows," one club executive reportedly said. Engle suited up for four games, but she never took the field. Her contract eventually was voided by minor league officials.

Major League Baseball commissioner Ford Frick, fearful that teams would use female players as publicity stunts, issued a ruling on June 21 banning women from the game.

World's Greatest Athlete *American Bob Mathias earned that distinction after trouncing the field in the decathlon at the 1952 Summer Olympics in Helsinki, Finland.*

Summer Olympics

Bob Mathias (b.1930) was the star for the United States in the Summer Olympic Games in Helsinki, Finland in July. The world's greatest athlete defended his 1948 gold medal by trouncing the field in the decathlon, winning by an astounding 912 points with a record total of 7,887.

Unlike four years earlier, when he was an unknown 17-year-old competing in only his third decathlon in London, Mathias was expected to become the first back-to-back decathlon gold medalist. He didn't disappoint, setting a world record and leading a gold-silver-bronze sweep for the United States in the event.

Medal Leaders: Summer Olympics

	GOLD	SILVER	BRONZE	TOTAL
USA	40	19	17	76
USSR	21	30	18	69
Hungary	16	10	16	42
Sweden	12	13	10	35
Germany	0	7	17	24

Rocky Marciano: Looks Can Be Deceiving

Rocky Marciano was not the textbook picture of a classic heavyweight champion. "Short, stoop-shouldered, balding...two left feet," his trainer Charley Goldman, once described him. "Rough and tough, but no finesse," trainer Goody Petronelli told *Sports Illustrated* in later years.

Marciano also had limited reach and was not particularly quick in the ring. But while he didn't look the part, Marciano had unbelievable desire, endurance, and an ability to withstand punishment. Those traits, plus a powerful right hand, carried him to 49 victories in 49 career fights. He's the only boxing champion to finish his career undefeated.

After a failed try at a professional baseball career, Marciano turned his attention to boxing full time in the late 1940s. He made an immediate impact, with nine first-round knockouts among his first 14 fights. A victory over heavyweight contender Roland LaStarza led to a match with former champion Joe Louis in 1951. When Marciano knocked him out, Louis retired for good (see page 14).

After Marciano won the heavyweight title in 1952, he successfully defended his crown half a dozen times before a back injury forced him to retire at 31 years old in 1956. He died in a plane crash in 1969, one day before his 46th birthday.

Other American gold medalists at the Games included middleweight boxer Floyd Patterson (b.1935), sprinter Lindy Remigino (the surprise winner in the 100 meters), and Horace Ashenfelter, an FBI agent who set an Olympic record in the 3,000-meter steeplechase.

Internationally, the Games were notable because they included a team from the Soviet Union for the first time. The USSR finished second to the United States with 21 gold medals (the Americans had 40) and with 69 total medals (the Americans had 76).

The international star, however, came from Czechoslovakia. Distance runner Emil Zatopek (b.1922) won the 5,000- and 10,000-meter races in world-record time, then entered the marathon, an event he had never run before. He won that, too, with his nearest rival finishing half a mile behind. His time was more than six minutes better than any previous Olympic gold medalist in the event. Zatopek's wife, Dana, won a gold medal in the javelin on the same day he won the 5,000 meters.

Television Expands Its Reach

The sports world was continuing to open its eyes to the incredible reach of the relatively new medium of television. The year marked college football's first foray into national television.

On New Year's day, Big Ten-champion University of Illinois capped a 9–0–1 season with a 40–7 drubbing of Pacific Coast Conference winner Stanford University. NBC telecast the game to the entire nation—a first for college football.

Then, in June, the NCAA approved a referendum permitting weekly national telecasts beginning with the 1952 season. But the organization voted to limit schools to one appearance per season. The University of Notre Dame, which a half century later had a network contract all to itself, thought that wasn't right. Rev. John J. Cavanaugh, Notre Dame's president, complained that the rule was "illegal and unfairly restricts an institution's right to televise."

Dropo's Dozen

Walt Dropo was a 6-foot-5, 220-pound behemoth of a major league first baseman who once was offered a contract by the NFL's Chicago Bears.

Though Dropo belted 152 home runs in his career—including 34 for the Boston Red Sox in 1950—he is best remembered for a torrid hitting stretch in the summer of 1952.

On June 3, Dropo was sent to the Detroit Tigers as part of a nine-player trade. On July 14th, the slugger hit five singles in Detroit's 8-2 victory over the New York Yankees.

As it turned out, Dropo was only getting warmed up. The next day, he went 4-for-4 in the first game of a doubleheader against the Washington Senators. In the second game, he had hits his first three times at bat.

Dropo was just a .270 career hitter. But his 12 consecutive hits those two days tied a major league record that still stands.

Series Sluggers

Mickey Mantle's decisive home run in game six of the World Series (page 32) was the first of his record 18 career homers in the Series. The all-time leaders (through 2002):

Mickey Mantle	18
Babe Ruth	15
Yogi Berra	12
Duke Snider	11
Reggie Jackson	10
Lou Gehrig	10
Joe DiMaggio	8

Fight Night in Philadelphia

Things got off to a bad start for Rocky Marciano in his heavyweight title fight against champion Jersey Joe Walcott (1914–1994) on September 23 at Philadelphia's Municipal Stadium. Marciano, who was 42–0 with 37 knockouts in his career at the time, was knocked down in the first round with the "hardest punch I ever took."

Marciano had never been sent to the mat before, and he apparently didn't like it there. He immediately bounced back up and the fight went on. It didn't get a whole lot better for the challenger, though, who was battered and bruised and trailing on each of the judges' scorecards through 12 rounds.

Told by his corner that he needed a knockout, Marciano went after the champ in the 13th round. He backed Walcott into a corner, sized him up, then delivered a brutal right punch that left the champion clinging with one arm to the ropes. Marciano followed with a left, and Walcott was down. And out. Marciano had a knockout and the heavyweight title.

1952

Wait 'til Next Year

"Wait 'til next year," fans of baseball's Brooklyn Dodgers were fond of saying after their team repeatedly came tantalizingly close to a World Series title. In 1952, "next year" looked as if it finally had arrived. But Mickey Mantle and Billy Martin (1928–1989) came to the rescue for the New York Yankees, who won their fourth consecutive World Series in October.

Brooklyn, still in search of its first championship, took a three-games-to-two lead with the final two games scheduled at home at Ebbets Field. The Dodgers led 1–0 in game six until a home run by Yogi Berra (b.1925) tied it. Mantle's homer in the eighth was the difference in New York's 3–2 win.

Mantle homered again the next day to break a 2–2 tie in the sixth inning. It was 4–2 in the seventh when Martin made the play of the series. Brooklyn had the bases loaded with one out and Jackie Robinson at the plate. Robinson hit a seemingly innocent little popup on the field, but first baseman Joe Collins looked up and lost the ball in the sun. Pitcher Bob Kuzava stood transfixed on the mound. Martin, the second baseman, realized that no one was going for the ball. It looked as if the ball might fall onto the field—with disastrous results for the Yankees. He sprinted in and made a game-saving knee-high catch between the pitcher's mound and first base.

That was it for the Dodgers. Kuzava got out of the inning and got Brooklyn out in the eighth and the ninth to save it.

The AAGPBL: The Ladies' Turn at Bat

"There's no crying in baseball!" Actor Tom Hanks (b.1956) didn't utter those immortal words until 1992, in the movie *A League of Their Own*. But Hanks' movie depicted life in the All-American Girls Professional Baseball League, which was started nearly half a century earlier.

Cubs owner Philip K. Wrigley (1894–1977), who was looking for alternative ways to fill major league stadiums while more and more young men were headed overseas for World War II, had a large part in the origins of the league, which began play in 1943. Teams were located in four cities not far from the league headquarters in Chicago: Racine, Wisconsin; Kenosha, Wisconsin; Rockford, Illinois; and South Bend, Indiana.

The league quickly grew to include more teams and more players, many of whom were managed by former big-league stars such as Bill Wambsganss and Jimmie Foxx. The AAGPBL's heyday came in the late-1940s, when more than 900,000 fans paid to watch its 10 teams play. But with the men back from the military and more and more big-league games on television, interest in the women's game waned. Franchises began to fail in the early 1950s. By 1952, the league was back down to only six teams. Two seasons later, the AAGPBL folded.

Other Milestones of 1952

✔ Kansas's basketball team completed a 26–2 season with an easy 80–63 victory over St. John's in the NCAA title game March 26 in Seattle. Kansas center Clyde Lovellette scored 33 points in the final.

✔ Montreal's Maurice "Rocket" Richard became the NHL's all-time leading goal scorer when he put number 325 into the net in a game against the Chicago Black Hawks on November 8.

✔ The Detroit Red Wings allowed only two goals in a four-game sweep of the Montreal Canadiens in hockey's Stanley Cup finals in April.

✔ The LPGA's Patty Berg shot a women's record 64 in the opening round of the Richmond Open golf tournament on April 26.

✔ Twenty-two-year-old Troy Ruttman won the Indianapolis 500 auto race on May 30 when leader Billy Vukovich crashed with nine laps to go.

Dick "Night Train" Lane intercepts a pass.

✔ Rams rookie Dick "Night Train" Lane set an NFL record that still stands by intercepting 14 passes in 1952. Lane got his nickname from Buddy Morrow's big-band hit tune of the same name in the early 1950s.

The Dodgers lost in the World Series for the sixth time in six tries.

Lion Kings

Statistically, the Cleveland Browns dominated the Detroit Lions in the 1952 NFL championship game December 28 in Cleveland. On the scoreboard, however, the Lions prevailed 17–7.

Behind the running of Harry Jagade and Marion Motley and the passing of Otto Graham, the Browns amassed large advantages in first downs (22–10) and total yards (384–258). But, except for Jagade's seven-yard touchdown run in the third quarter, Cleveland could not finish its drives. Detroit's key defensive stand came after Motley ran 54 yards to the Lions' five-yard line with the Browns trailing just 14–7 early in the fourth quarter. Motley and Graham took big losses on the next two plays, and Cleveland did not score.

Bobby Layne (1926–1986) ran two yards for a touchdown in the second quarter and Doak Walker (1927–1998) had a 67-yard touchdown burst in the third quarter to help Detroit build a 14–0 lead. Pat Harder added an insurance field goal in the fourth quarter. The Lions won their first title in 17 years, while the Browns lost in the championship game for the second consecutive season.

1953

Cousy Makes Headlines, but the Lakers Win Another Title

Bob Cousy (b.1928) became the first player to score 50 points in an NBA playoff game when he reached that mark in the Boston Celtics' four-overtime victory over the Syracuse Nationals on March 21. Cousy made only 10 baskets but sank 30 of his 32 free throws, including five in the final overtime period, to help Boston secure a 111–105 win.

Cousy's heroics helped Boston clinch the opening round, two games to none. The Celtics lost in the next round, the division finals, to the New York Knickerbockers. The Knicks, though, still couldn't break through for their first title. After beating the Minneapolis Lakers in game one of the finals, the Lakers roared back in April to sweep the last four games and capture their fourth championship in five seasons.

Marciano Makes Short Work of Walcott

When Rocky Marciano and Jersey Joe Walcott fought for the first time in 1952 (see page 31), it was a tough fight not decided until Marciano, trailing on all the judges' cards, knocked out the heavyweight champion in the 13th round. The rematch was neither as lengthy nor as dramatic. Marciano defended his title with little trouble, knocking out the ex-champ in the first round on May 15.

The fight was not without controversy, however. After a powerful combination of punches sent Walcott to the mat in the opening round, Jersey Joe propped himself up on one knee and appeared alert and coherent. "I could have gotten up at the count of three," he told the media afterward, adding that he was not hurt at any time. But Walcott stayed on one knee a split second too long. The referee counted 10, and Marciano was still the heavyweight champion. It was the 38-year-old Walcott's last fight. He retired soon afterward.

On Top of the World

Edmund Hillary (b.1919) and Tenzing Norgay (1914–1986) were the first mountaineers to reach the top of Mt. Everest, when they arrived at the summit on May 29. Hillary, from New Zealand, and Norgay, his Nepalese Sherpa guide, were

Little Mo's Big Feat *Maureen Connolly (leaping) became the first woman to win tennis' Grand Slam.*

part of an Everest expedition organized by John Hunt of Great Britain.

Little Mo's Grand Slam

Eighteen-year-old Maureen Connolly completed an amazing sweep of tennis' major championships when she won the singles title at the U.S. Open on September 7. Connolly beat Doris Hart 6–2, 6–4 in the final at Forest Hills in New York.

Earlier in the year, the player known as "Little Mo" surged to victories at Wimbledon and in the French and Australian Opens. She was the first woman

1953

(and only the second person) to win all four titles in the same year, a Grand Slam that previously only had been accomplished by Don Budge (1915–2000).

Hart also was Connolly's final-round victim at the French Open and Wimbledon. In all, Connolly won 22 matches without a loss in the four Grand Slam tournaments. Incredibly, she lost just one set in her record run.

Yankee Slugger *New York Yankees outfielder Mickey Mantle awed baseball fans with his tape-measure home runs, including a legendary blast at Washington's Griffith Stadium.*

Mantle's Prodigious Blast

Washington Senators left-hander Chuck Stobbs wound and threw. Mickey Mantle uncoiled a mighty swing and, as he had many times before and after, sent the ball on a deep arc toward the leftfield fence. Only this time, it seemed as if the ball was not going to come down. The crowd at Griffith Stadium in Washington that April 17 gasped as Mantle's gargantuan home run easily cleared the stands beyond the fence, caromed off the corner of the football scoreboard, and disappeared outside the stadium.

There were no computerized estimates of how far the ball traveled (as there routinely are today). But Yankees officials guessed the ball went 565 feet, at least 460 of that in the air. The tape-measure home run captured the attention of baseball fans everywhere—and of pitchers all over the American League.

Holloman's Good Start

Bobo Holloman had little success as a relief pitcher for the lowly St. Louis Browns early in the 1953 season. Holloman begged for a chance to be a starting pitcher, however, and Browns manager Marty Marion obliged, sending the 29-year-old to the mound on May 6 against the Philadelphia Athletics.

Fewer than 2,500 people were in the stands on that rainy night in St. Louis (ironically, Holloman had already had two starts washed out by rain). What the fans in attendance saw, though, was one of the more unlikely pitching gems in Major

Mickey Mantle:
DiMaggio's Worthy Successor

Young Mickey Mantle came along in the 1950s and took his place among the pantheon of Yankee legends that includes Babe Ruth, Lou Gehrig, Yogi Berra, and Joe DiMaggio (1914–1999).

Mantle had the good fortune and the bad luck to follow DiMaggio as the Yankees' full-time centerfielder—the good fortune because New York was in the midst of a record five-year run as world champions, and the bad luck because some fans felt Mantle could do nothing that would measure up to the great DiMaggio.

Mantle was only 21 when he became the Yankees' regular centerfielder in 1952, and he batted .311, was named to the American League all-star team, and finished third in the balloting for the league's most valuable player award that year. He was still only 25 when he won the Triple Crown in 1955, leading the league in home runs (52), RBI (130), and batting average (.353) while winning the first of back-to-back MVP awards. He helped the Yankees win the American League pennant 12 times in his 14 seasons.

And yet, it was not until the second half of his 18-year career—in 1961, after he fell short of the single-season home run record that teammate Roger Maris (1934–1985) eclipsed the same year—that he was fully embraced by Yankees fans. Once they did warm up to him, however, it was with unreserved fervor.

Mantle's talent for long home runs and his sprinter's speed were tempered only by a problem with alcohol and a succession of injuries, beginning with a severe knee injury suffered in the outfield during game two of the 1951 World Series. He retired following the 1968 season. In 18 years, he batted .298 with 536 home runs, more than any other switch-hitter in history. In 1974, the first year he was eligible, he was inducted into baseball's Hall of Fame.

Mantle died of cancer in 1995 at age 63.

League Baseball history. Holloman became only the third pitcher to toss a no-hitter in his first big-league start when he blanked the Athletics 6–0. For good measure, Holloman had the only two hits of his career and drove in three of the Browns' runs.

Holloman's no-hitter was hardly a classic. As he did throughout his brief major league career, Holloman struggled with his control. He walked five batters; another reached first base on Holloman's error. Several batters hit the ball hard, only to be thwarted by fine plays in the field.

In the ninth inning, the first two Athletics drew walks, but a double play left Holloman only one out from history. After another walk, Philadelphia's Eddie Robinson flied out to right field to end the game.

It's an understatement to say that Holloman pitched the best game of his career that night. He won only two other games and finished 3–7 with a 5.23 ERA in 1953. He allowed 50 walks in only 65.1 innings of work. Six days after Holloman's no-hitter, the Athletics got to him for three hits and a walk in only 1.1 innings. He was out of baseball for good less than three months after his no-hitter.

1953

Seventeen in One

Boston Red Sox Hall of Fame outfielder Ted Williams missed most of the 1953 season piloting a fighter jet in the Korean War (see page 28).

Without the "Splendid Splinter," the Red Sox offense suffered. Boston was near the bottom of the American League in home runs and runs scored, and finished 16 games behind the pennant-winning New York Yankees. But on June 18, the Red Sox put on a single-inning offensive display not seen before or since: Boston scored 17 runs in the seventh inning of a game against the Detroit Tigers. It was a modern record for runs in an inning, and still stands to this day.

The Red Sox, who had 20 hits in a 17–1 rout of Detroit a day earlier, took a 5–3 lead into the bottom of the seventh inning at Fenway Park. They proceeded to send 23 men to the plate—11 singled, two doubled, one homered, and six walked. All 17 runs were earned (they were not scored on errors). The final score of the game was 23–3.

Dick Gernet hit the lone home run in Boston's big seventh inning, and Sammy White and Tom Umphlett each reached base safely three times, but it was outfielder Gene Stephens who made history. He set an American League record by smacking three hits in the inning. Ironically, Stephens spent the majority of his big-league career as Williams' backup.

Tigers' pitcher Dick Gromek was the primary victim of the Red Sox' barrage. He allowed nine runs in the inning. But Gromek wasn't permanently scarred by the disaster. He shut out the Athletics, 5–0, five days later at Philadelphia's Shibe Park, and went on to win 18 games for the Tigers the following season.

Golf's Major League

Golf's legends are defined by their performance in the major championships. Ben Hogan's three major titles in 1953 highlighted a remarkable run of nine victories in the 16 majors that he entered from 1946 to 1953. The all-time leaders in major championships (through 2002):

Jack Nicklaus	18
Bobby Jones	13
Walter Hagen	11
Ben Hogan	9
Gary Player	9
Arnold Palmer	8
Tom Watson	8
Tiger Woods	8

The current majors are the Masters, U.S. Open, British Open, and PGA Championship. The U.S. Amateur and British Amateur have been considered majors in the past.

The "Wee Ice Mon" Wins in Scotland

Perhaps no other American golfer had ever been as revered across the Atlantic as legendary Ben Hogan, who played in his only British Open at

Carnoustie, Scotland, in July. The fans there called him the "Wee Ice Mon," and they cheered him on to a relatively easy four-stroke victory in the Open.

Easy on the scoreboard, that is. But the brutal weather at Carnoustie made things difficult on Hogan, who physically was never the same after his near-fatal car accident in 1949 (see page 13). Wind, rain, cold, hail, and the flu, which Hogan contracted before the 36-hole final day, all converged on him. He shot a 70 for the morning's 18 holes to tie for the overall lead. In the afternoon, his 68 set a new course record and left him well ahead of the pack.

Hogan's victory at Carnoustie capped an amazing year in which he entered only six events and won five of them (he finished third in the other). He won the Masters and the U.S. Open before capping his major run with the British Open. No golfer before or since has won all three in the same year.

Hogan's limited schedule was the result of the lingering effects of the accident. After winning the British Open, he was so exhausted that he took the rest of the year off, passing a chance to complete a Grand Slam at the season's fourth and final major, the PGA Championship.

When Hogan returned home from Carnoustie, he rode the streets of Manhattan in a ticker-tape parade in his honor.

Lew Worsham's Timely Eagle

"It was the luckiest shot I ever had in my life," Lew Worsham said after knocking his ball into the hole from the 18th fairway to win the Tam O'Shanter World Championship in Chicago in August.

Worsham couldn't have picked a better time for his good fortune—neither for himself nor for golf. The Tam O'Shanter was the richest tournament on the PGA Tour, and its winner's share was an unheard-of $25,000. The huge purse attracted television's interest, and the 1953 event was the first live, national telecast of a golf tournament. What more than 1 million people saw on television was a million-to-one shot.

Worsham trailed leader Chandler Harper by one stroke heading into the final hole and needed a birdie three (one stroke under par) to force a playoff. Worsham's first shot left him about 115 yards from the hole. He pulled out a wedge and landed his shot near the front of the green, about 45 feet away. The ball bounced once, twice, three times, then rolled into the cup for an incredible eagle (two strokes under par)! He had won the tournament by one stroke.

Another Classic Fall for the Dodgers

The Yankees added to the Dodgers' frustration by winning the World Series again from their Brooklyn neighbors. New York's six-game victory was its record fifth championship in a row, while the Dodgers lost the World Series for the seventh time in as many trips to the Fall Classic in October. It was the fifth time Brooklyn fell to the Yankees, and the second year in a row. Also for the second year in a row, scrappy second baseman

Other Milestones of 1953

✔ Among college football's New Year's day bowl games: University of Alabama blasted University of Syracuse 61–6 in the Orange Bowl, setting a postseason record for points, and University of Southern California beat University of Wisconsin 7–0 in the Rose Bowl, marking the first time that a Pacific Coast Conference team beat the Big 10 representative since the conferences began their annual game in 1947.

✔ After 77 years in Boston, baseball's Braves packed their bags only weeks before the start of the 1953 season and moved to Milwaukee on March 18.

✔ Indiana capped a 23–3 season by edging defending-champion Kansas 69–68 to win the NCAA basketball title in March.

✔ The Montreal Canadiens, runners-up the previous two years, beat the Boston Bruins in five games to win hockey's Stanley Cup in April.

✔ Long shot Dark Star was the surprise winner over favored Native Dancer in horse racing's Kentucky Derby on May 2. Jockey Hank Moreno was aboard the winner. Native Dancer, ridden by jockey Eric Guerin, came back to win the Preakness and the Belmont.

Native Dancer

✔ After a near miss the previous year, when he crashed late in the race, Bill Vukovich won the Indianapolis 500 auto race for the first time on May 30.

✔ With Ben Hogan not in the field, Walter Burkemo won golf's PGA Championship in August. It was the lone major that Hogan did not win in 1953.

✔ Tony Trabert won his first singles tennis title at the U.S. Open in Forest Hills on September 7.

Billy Martin was one of the heroes for New York.

Martin's hit broke a 3–3 tie in the bottom of the ninth inning of game six and drove in the winning run. The winning hit capped a brilliant series for Martin. He tripled in three runs in his first at-bat in game one and went on to hit .500 with a team-leading eight RBI. His 12 hits set a record for a six-game World Series.

The Dodgers were dominant during the regular season, going 105–49 and winning the National League pennant by a whopping 13 games over second-place Milwaukee. Things got off to a bad start for Brooklyn in the World Series, though, when 20-game winner Carl Erskine (b.1926) did not get past the first inning in the Yankees' 9–5 victory.

With the Dodgers down two games to none, Erskine came back to win game three two days later—he struck out a record 14 Yankees in a 3–2 victory—and Brooklyn evened the series with another win in game four. But Mickey Mantle's grand slam home run highlighted New York's 11–7 win in the fifth game, and Martin's single decided game six.

Layne's Quick Thinking Lifts Lions

Quarterback Bobby Layne's arm—and his head—helped lift the Detroit Lions past the Cleveland Browns in the NFL championship game for the second consecutive season on December 27.

Doak Walker's one-yard touchdown run and his 23-yard field goal gave the Lions a 10–3 halftime lead in the game at Detroit's Briggs Stadium. But Cleveland rallied to tie the game at 10–10 on Harry "Chick" Jagade's nine-yard touchdown run in the third quarter, then took a six-point lead when Lou Groza kicked a pair of field goals in the fourth period.

But Layne marched his team from its 20-yard line to Cleveland's 33-yard line with just over two minutes remaining. After calling a time out to talk things over, the Lions decided to go with a screen pass (a short pass to one side of the field which a receiver then carries downfield behind a screen of blockers) on the next play to counter the Browns' fierce pass rush.

In the huddle, though, Layne changed the call. He reasoned that Cleveland would be concentrating on end Cloyce Box, as it had been all day, instead of end Jim Doran, who was normally a backup. Plus, "Doran had been begging me to throw deep all day," Layne said later.

So Layne used Box as a decoy. He had him run a short pattern to draw in the defense, then lofted a high pass to a streaking Doran in the right corner of the end zone. Doran grabbed it for a touchdown, and the Lions held on to win 17–16.

Doran, who was on the field only because starting end Leon Hart was injured earlier in the game, was an unlikely star. He caught only six passes for 75 yards during the regular season, but he had three receptions for 68 yards on the winning drive alone. Layne passed for 179 yards and ran for 46.

Meanwhile, Browns quarterback Otto Graham had the worst game, statistically at least, of his brilliant career. He completed only two of 15 passes for 20 yards, was intercepted twice, and lost a fumble that led to Detroit's first touchdown in the first quarter.

NFL Champs

The Lions won three NFL championships in the 1950s, but they haven't won any titles since. The decade's NFL champions:

1950	Cleveland Browns
1951	Los Angeles Rams
1952	Detroit Lions
1953	Detroit Lions
1954	Cleveland Browns
1955	Cleveland Browns
1956	New York Giants
1957	Detroit Lions
1958	Baltimore Colts
1959	Baltimore Colts

1954

Tackle Can't Stop Moegle

In college football, during the January 1 Cotton Bowl, Rice University halfback Dicky Moegle took a handoff at his team's five-yard line, burst through the line of scrimmage, and headed down the right sideline with nothing but daylight between him and goal line. He figured he was well on his way to a 95-yard touchdown run when a flash of a red University of Alabama jersey came from seemingly out of nowhere and dropped Moegle at the Alabama 40-yard line.

Unfortunately for Alabama, that tackle was by Tommy Lewis—who was not in the game at the time. Lewis, unable to contain himself at the sight of an opponent running down a clear field, leaped from the sideline to make the play. "I didn't know what I was doing," he said after the game. "I kept telling myself I didn't do it, I didn't do it. But I knew I did."

The officials knew, too. Lewis was sent back to the sideline, and Moegle was awarded a touchdown. He already had a 79-yard scoring run to his credit and later added a 34-yard touchdown. He finished the game with 265 rushing yards and three touchdowns. Rice won 28–6.

Selvy Scores 100

Furman University's Frank Selvy scored an NCAA-record 100 points in the Paladins' 149–95 victory over Newberry College on February 13. Selvy made 41 of 66 shots and added 18 free-throws in the game at Greenville, South Carolina.

By season's end, the Furman star scored 50 or more points in eight games. He led the nation by averaging a record 41.7 points per game.

A Short Storybook

When Joe DiMaggio and Marilyn Monroe (1926–1962) began their courtship in 1952, the public was captivated. It was a storybook romance between a legendary baseball hero and the biggest, most alluring star on the screen. On January 14, the two were married in a civil ceremony in San Francisco, DiMaggio's hometown.

The marriage never had a chance, though. DiMaggio, who retired after the 1951 season, was a quiet and reserved man, and preferred to remain out of the public eye. He wanted a family. Monroe attracted attention wherever she went.

Diamonds Aren't Forever *The storybook marriage of Joe DiMaggio and Marilyn Monroe had an unhappy ending.*

She wanted a career. Less than nine months after their marriage, she filed for divorce.

It was apparent from the start that the two were not suited as husband and wife. While they were on on their honeymoon in Japan, Monroe was asked to detour to Korea to entertain the American troops. DiMaggio didn't like the idea, but Monroe went. When she returned, she was ecstatic. "Joe, you've never heard such cheering," she said.

1954

To which DiMaggio, who had been adored by tens of thousands of fans every time he stepped to plate at Yankee Stadium, replied, "Yes, I have."

Stan the Man's Home Run Barrage

St. Louis Cardinals outfielder Stan Musial (b.1920) was a seven-time batting champion who hit an amazing .331 in his 22-year career. He also hit 475 home runs, and on May 2 he put on one of the greatest slugging exhibitions in baseball history. In a doubleheader in St. Louis against the New York Giants, Musial hit a record five home runs. No other player had hit more than four homers in a single day.

"Stan the Man's" day began with a walk his first time up in game one. But he homered in the third, fifth, and eighth innings, the last one a three-run blast off reliever Jim Hearn to break a 6–6 tie and spark St. Louis to a 10–6 victory. In the second game, Musial homered twice more off Giants knuckleball pitcher Hoyt Wilhelm (1923–2002), although New York won the game 9–7.

Musial's totals for the day: six hits in eight at-bats, five home runs, and nine RBI.

Evolution of the Mile Record (1900–1954)

4:15.4	John Paul Jones, United States	1911
4:14.4	John Paul Jones, United States	1913
4:12.6	Norman Taber, United States	1915
4:10.4	Paavo Nurmi, Finland	1923
4:09.2	Jules Ladoumegue, France	1931
4:07.6	Jack Lovelock, New Zealand	1933
4:06.8	Glenn Cunningham, United States	1934
4:06.4	Sydney Wooderson, Britain	1937
4:06.2	Gunder Haegg, Sweden	1942
4:06.2	Arne Andersson, Sweden	1942
4:04.6	Gunder Haegg, Sweden	1942
4:02.6	Arne Andersson, Sweden	1943
4:01.6	Arne Andersson, Sweden	1944
4:01.4	Gunder Haegg, Sweden	1945
3:59.4	Roger Bannister, Britain	1954

Bannister Runs a Miracle Mile

Certain numbers are magical in sports: 3,000 hits, 20 wins, 1,000 yards rushing, a four-minute mile. For a long time, no one thought that last mark was attainable. But on May 7, Oxford University medical student Roger Bannister (b.1929) broke the tape in three minutes and 59.4 seconds on his home track in England.

"Naturally, I wanted to have a try at it," said Bannister, who decided just minutes before the race to push for the mark. That's because the sun came out shortly before race time, and the day's wind and cold rain ceased.

Many people believed American miler Wes Santee would be the first to break the four-minute mark in the mile. As it turned out, not only did Bannister beat everyone, but the first American to accomplish the feat was Don Bowden, who didn't do it until 1957.

Just in case there were any doubts surrounding Bannister's feat, surveyors took to the track after the race and validated the distance. In fact, they found that four laps around the Oxford track came out to one mile . . . plus half an inch!

Zaharias' Big Comeback

Babe Didrikson Zaharias (1914–1956) experienced perhaps her greatest triumph when she won the U.S. Women's Open in golf at Salem Country Club in Peabody, Massachusetts, in July. Zaharias won by a whopping 12 strokes. "The Babe has now completely outclassed all her challengers," Al Laney wrote in the *New York Herald Tribune*.

It was not simply the margin of victory that Laney was referring to, nor was that what made the win her greatest and made it an inspiration to legions of sports fans. It was because Zaharias' victory came despite a fight with cancer that had required surgery only a year earlier.

The grueling 72 holes of the Open, including 36 on the last day, finally began to catch up to Zaharias at the end. Still, she finished with a four-day total of 291—well ahead of all her competitors.

A Champion Babe *Babe Didrikson Zaharias hoists the trophy after capturing golf's 1954 U.S. Women's Open. For more on this outstanding and multitalented athlete, see the box on the next page.*

Indians Dethrone Yankees

The New York Yankees won 103 games during baseball's regular season, but for once the pinstripers weren't good enough. While 103 victories usually will win a pennant, New York finished a distant eight games behind the Cleveland Indians, who won a record 111 games against only 43 losses. The Yankees' five-year streak as world champions finally came to an end.

The Indians fashioned their record-setting season behind a dominant pitching staff, which was led by Bob Lemon (1920–2000) and Early Wynn (1920–1999), with 23 wins apiece. Teammate Mike Garcia led the league with a 2.64 ERA while winning 19 of 27 decisions. Bob Feller (b.1918) won 13 games while making only 19 starts.

Cleveland led the league in most pitching categories, but the Indians had plenty of muscle at the plate, too. They were tops in home runs with 156, including a league-leading 32 homers by out-

1954

fielder Larry Doby (b.1923). Second baseman Bobby Avila hit an American League-best .341.

Cleveland started the season 3–6, then reeled off six consecutive victories. Starting in mid-May, the Indians won 11 games in a row, and later had winning streaks of nine, eight, nine, and 11 games again.

The Catch

The Cleveland Indians, on the heels of their record 111 wins during the regular season, were heavily favored to beat the New York Giants in the World Series. As it turned out, the October Series was a rout—but not by the Indians. The Giants swept in four games.

For all intents and purposes, the Series was over on the first day, September 29. Dusty Rhodes' pinch-hit, pop fly landed just over the 297-foot wall down the rightfield line to give New York a 5–2 win in 10 innings. But that wasn't what turned the Series the Giants' way. Instead, it was a brilliant play by centerfielder Willie Mays in the top of the eighth inning.

Mays was in just his third big-league season, and it already was clear that his talents were extraordinary. He could run, hit, and hit for power. But the signature play of this Series—indeed, the signa-

Babe Didrikson Zaharias:
The Greatest Female Athlete

There may never have been a greater female athlete than Babe Didrikson Zaharias, who could do just about anything she wanted to on a playing field.

When she was 18, Zaharias (she was Babe Didrikson then, before her marriage to pro wrestler George Zaharias) won two gold medals and a silver in track and field at the 1932 Olympics in Los Angeles. She also was a star in basketball, tennis, bowling, and volleyball, and she once pitched an inning in a Major League Baseball spring training game. Another time, she reportedly struck out Joe DiMaggio in an exhibition.

When Zaharias decided she would concentrate on golf, she became one of the greatest golfers in history. Zaharias was so dominant that from 1946 to 1947, she won 17 consecutive tournaments.

While Zaharias undoubtedly was naturally talented, it was her relentless desire that truly set her apart from her peers. That desire helped carry her to her greatest triumph at the U.S. Women's Open in 1954. It came just a year after cancer surgery.

"When I was in the hospital, I prayed that I could play again," Zaharias said. She not only returned to the links, she still played at a level higher than anyone else. Less than four months after her surgery, Zaharias returned to competition. Her resounding victory in the U.S. Open was her fourth win since leaving the hospital.

In the end, Zaharias succumbed to cancer. She was just 42 when she died in 1956. She remains the greatest all-around female athlete in history.

Other Milestones of 1954

✔ Despite starting the race from the 19th position, Bill Vukovich successfully defended his Indianapolis 500 auto race championship with an easy victory over second-place finisher Jimmy Bryan on Memorial Day.

✔ Tom Gola, the college player of the year, led La Salle College to the NCAA basketball championship. La Salle beat Bradley University 92–76 in the championship game in Kansas City on March 20.

Bill Vukovich

✔ Tony Leswick's overtime hockey goal on April 16 gave the Detroit Red Wings a 2–1 victory over the Montreal Canadiens in the seventh and deciding game of the Stanley Cup finals.

✔ The Minneapolis Lakers beat the Syracuse Nationals in seven games to win the NBA title for the third consecutive year and the fifth time in six seasons. The dynasty soon ended, though, because dominating center George Mikan, at age 30, retired.

ture play of his career—came from his glove.

With the score tied at 2–2, the Indians put their first two runners on base to lead off the eighth inning. First baseman Vic Wertz lined a drive to the deepest part of the Polo Grounds in centerfield. Mays knew the ball was over his head. But he also knew that the Polo Grounds had nearly 450 feet before you got to the wall to the right of center. He turned and ran for the wall.

At the last instant, Mays put his glove up over his shoulder and made the catch with his back to the wall. Then he suddenly stopped his sprint, whirled, and threw the ball back to the infield. The runners had to hold at first and second base; the Indians did not score.

In the 10th inning, it was Mays who started the winning rally by walking with one out and stealing second base. But his biggest play didn't come at bat or on the base paths. It came more than 425 feet from home plate.

The Browns Back on Top

After losing three straight NFL Championship Games, the Cleveland Browns were back on top again with a 56–10 rout of the Detroit Lions in the title game on December 26.

The Browns jumped to a 21–3 lead early in the second quarter and built a 35–10 advantage by halftime. Quarterback Otto Graham, who said it was his last game, passed for three touchdowns and ran for three touchdowns. Cleveland's defense intercepted six passes and recovered three fumbles.

Graham completed nine of 12 passes for 163 yards and one touchdown. Graham's scoring runs came from one yard, five yards, and one yard. After the game, he retired. He meant it, too. But by training camp the next year, Browns coach Paul Brown, desperate for one more season out of his star quarterback, talked him out of retirement. Cleveland went on to win another title in 1955.

1955

Hockey Town, U.S.A.

The Detroit Red Wings beat the Montreal Canadiens in seven games to win the NHL's Stanley Cup in April. Detroit won the deciding game 3–1. Gordie Howe's (b.1928) goal 11 seconds before the end of the second period proved to be the game winner. The Canadiens were playing without star winger Maurice Richard (1921– 2000), who was suspended by league president Clarence Campbell for his role in a fight in Boston one month earlier. One day after he suspended the NHL's all-time leading goal scorer, Campbell's presence at a Canadiens–Red Wings game in Montreal sparked a riot inside and outside the Montreal Forum.

After Detroit's title, only one team from the United States (the Chicago Black Hawks in 1961) won the Stanley Cup until 1970.

O Canada

With 10 NHL titles, the Detroit Red Wings have won the Stanley Cup more times than any other team in the United States. They're third among all NHL teams, behind the Montreal Canadiens and the Toronto Maple Leafs. The all-time leaders:

TEAM	CHAMPIONSHIPS
Montreal Canadiens	23
Toronto Maple Leafs	13
Detroit Red Wings	10
Boston Bruins	5
Edmonton Oilers	5

Time Is on Syracuse's Side in the NBA Finals

The Syracuse Nationals beat the Ft. Wayne Pistons 92–91 in game seven of the NBA finals on April 10, putting a thrilling exclamation point on a revolutionary season. The victory was particularly sweet for Syracuse owner Danny Biasone, whose idea to add a shot clock (a limit on how long a team could control the ball without taking a shot) revitalized pro basketball—and may have saved his team from defeat in the final game.

With fans becoming restless at stalling tactics and foul-plagued games, the NBA instituted the 24-second shot clock and

Next Year Is Here *Sandy Amoros slides in to score during the Dodgers' World Series triumph (page 52).*

the bonus free throw rule for the 1954–55 season. "Pro basketball would not have survived without a [shot] clock," Biasone said.

That assessment was validated by increased fan interest in a season that featured an increase of more than 13 points per team per game. The Boston Celtics became the first team in NBA history to average more than 100 points per game for a season, although Syracuse ousted the Celtics three-games-to-one for the division title.

In the deciding game of the finals, Ft. Wayne bolted to a 17-point lead in the second quarter. "Under the old rules, they'd have gone into a stall," Biasone said. Instead, the Nationals chipped away and eked out a one-point victory. George King's free throw with 12 seconds left provided the winning margin, and his steal in the closing seconds secured the win.

1955

Elston Howard Dons the Pinstripes

In 1955 Rosa Parks, a black woman in Montgomery, Alabama, refused to give up her seat to a white man on a city bus, sparking a civil-rights movement that led to sweeping changes.

While Major League Baseball had been integrated for nearly a decade by the 1950s, African-American players still often took a back seat to their white counterparts. By the middle of the decade, four big-league teams—most notably, the powerful New York Yankees—still were not integrated.

The Yankees finally called up their first African-American player to the parent club in 1955. Elston Howard (1929–1980), a burly catcher who bided his time in the outfield while Yogi Berra still was in the prime of his career, made his debut in pinstripes on April 14. He singled in his first at-bat during New York's 8-4 victory over the Boston Red Sox.

Howard batted .274 and slugged 167 home runs in his 14-year career. He was an American League all-star nine consecutive years, from 1957-1965, and played in the postseason 10 times. Ironically, Howard finished his career with the Red Sox in 1968. Only nine years earlier, Boston had become the last major league team to integrate.

Roberto Clemente Makes His Big-League Debut

Puerto Rican native Roberto Clemente (1934–1972) broke into the major leagues with the Pittsburgh Pirates on April 17, and made inroads for Latin American players and others from around the world.

Although Clemente hit a modest .255 that season, it quickly became apparent that he possessed remarkable defensive skills and an uncanny ability to hit. He batted .311 in 1956, and won four batting titles in an 18-year career in which he batted .317 in all. He also led the National League in outfield assists four times, and he won 12 consecutive Gold Glove Awards.

Clemente's final hit of the 1972 season was the 3,000th of his illustrious career. It also was his last. Tragically, Clemente died in a plane crash that New Year's Eve while helping to bring relief supplies to the victims of a devastating earthquake in Nicaragua.

A short time later, the mandatory five-year waiting period for the Baseball Hall of Fame was waived—the first and only time since Lou Gehrig (1903–1941)—and Clemente was elected on a whopping 93 percent of the ballots.

Clemente not only was the first Latino Hall of Famer, but he also helped to open doors for scores of international players to follow. Today, major-league baseball rosters are dotted with players from all over the world.

Tragedy at the Indy 500

Bill Sweikert won the Indianapolis 500 auto race on Memorial Day, May 30, but the celebration was tempered by the death of two-time defending champion Bill Vukovich (1918–1955) on the track. Vukovich, who was called the "Mad Russian" for his hard-charging style, was just 36 years old when he died.

Vukovich was leading more than halfway through his bid for a record third consecutive Indy 500 win when he approached an accident on the track. He had only a small space in which to pass the multi-car wreck, and couldn't get by cleanly. His car flew over the wall, crashed on its nose, bounced, and burst into flames. He died of a skull fracture before the flames got him.

Horse of the Year *Jockey Eddie Arcaro rode Nashua to only one loss in 1955. His victories included record runs in the Preakness and Belmont stakes, and a great match race with rival horse Swaps.*

Surprise Winner in U.S. Open Playoff

Jack Fleck, a municipal golf pro from Davenport, Iowa, won the U.S. Open in an 18-hole playoff with Ben Hogan on June 19 at the Olympic Club in San Francisco. Fleck was one of the mot unlikely winners ever. He tied Hogan with a final-round 67 on Saturday, including a birdie (one shot under par) on the 72nd, and final, hole.

Surprisingly, the unheralded Fleck was in control over the legendary Hogan all the way in the Sunday playoff. Fleck never trailed, finished the first nine holes in 33 (two shots under par), and cruised to a three-shot victory.

The ultimate irony? Fleck was playing with a new set of clubs manufactured by Hogan's company.

Nashua and Swaps Go One-on-One

The biggest horse race of 1955 wasn't the Kentucky Derby. Nor was it one of the other legs of Thoroughbred racing's Triple Crown. Instead, it was a match race on August 31 at Washington Park in Chicago: Nashua versus Swaps in a $100,000, winner-take-all race over 1 1/4 miles. A national television audience eagerly tuned in to see once and for all which was the better horse.

The seeds for the match race were sown when jockey Bill Shoemaker (b.1931) rode Swaps to an upset of the favored Nashua, ridden by jockey Eddie Arcaro (b.1916), in the Kentucky Derby. With Swaps not entered in the next two stages of the Triple Crown—the Preakness and the Belmont Stakes—Nashua dominated. He set a record in the Preakness, then won by nine lengths in the Belmont.

The match race turned out to be a mismatch. Swaps was the heavy favorite, but Nashua never trailed. Swaps stayed close enough, though, and came out of

1955

the final turn only a couple of lengths behind.

Shoemaker pushed his horse to make a move, but to no avail. Nashua pulled away with every stride in the homestretch and won easily, by six-and-a-half lengths.

The match race defeat was the only loss for Swaps as a three-year-old. He had a dominant season in 1956 as a four-year-old. Nashua finished 1955 with only the one loss at the Kentucky Derby. He was named the Horse of the Year.

Winner and Still Champion *Rocky Marciano (right) beat Archie Moore in the last bout of his boxing career. Marciano remains the only heavyweight champ to retire undefeated.*

Rocky Goes Out on Top

Rocky Marciano defended his heavyweight crown one last time, knocking out challenger Archie Moore (1913–1998) in front of more than 61,000 fans at Yankee Stadium on September 21. Those fans did not know it then, but the fight would be Marciano's last. He retired the following April.

Moore, the light heavyweight champion, looked as if he might wrest the crown from Marciano when he started out strong and knocked the heavyweight champ to the mat in the second round. But Marciano dominated much of the fight after that. He knocked down Moore twice in the sixth round and again in the eighth. In the ninth round, a pair of blistering left hooks put the challenger down again. This time, it was for the count.

With the victory, Marciano improved his career record to 49–0. He was the fourth heavyweight to retire with the title, but the first three—James Jeffries (1875–1953), Gene Tunney (1898–1978), and Joe Louis—all came out of retirement to fight again. Marciano ruled out a return to boxing. "No man can say what he will do in the future," Marciano said. "But, barring poverty, the ring has seen the last of me."

Marciano had no financial problems, and he never fought again.

"Next Year" Arrives for Dodgers Fans

"Wait 'til next year," had been the cry of long-suffering Brooklyn fans for years, as their beloved Dodgers often came close to a World Series title, only to fall short. No need to wait until 1956, though. In its eighth World Series in 1955, Brooklyn finally won the elusive championship in October. What's more, the Dodgers' seven-game Series win came against their long-time bitter rivals, the New York Yankees.

For six games, the teams traded victories in their home parks: New York won the first two at Yankee Stadium; Brooklyn took the next three at Ebbets Field, and the Yankees evened the series with a win in game six in the Bronx. For the deciding game at Yankee Stadium, Brooklyn manager Walter Alston (1911–1984) picked left-hander Johnny Podres (b.1932) to start the game. His victory in game three had kept the Dodgers in the Series.

Brooklyn scratched out single runs in the fourth and the sixth innings before leftfielder Sandy Amoros (1930–1992) made the play of the Series in the bottom of the sixth. Amoros had just come into the game. In the top of the sixth, second baseman Don Zimmer (b.1931) was taken out for a pinch-hitter, and Junior Gilliam (1928–1978), who started in leftfield, moved to second base to replace him.

Otto Graham: Winning Is the Only Thing

Who is the greatest quarterback in NFL history? The question invariably draws a number of different answers, and the argument can never be settled. Some experts say Sammy Baugh (b.1914), the first of the great forward passers and an accomplished all-around player. Others say Joe Montana (b.1956), whose skill and grace may have been unparalleled. Then there's Johnny Unitas (1933–2002), a field general whose poise and presence inspired his troops. And Dan Marino (b.1961), a rifle-armed quarterback who posted the greatest statistics of any quarterback in history.

But if the criteria is winning, there has never been a more successful professional quarterback than Otto Graham. "By that standard, Otto was the best of them all," his head coach, Paul Brown, once said.

Brown was biased, to be sure, having coached Graham in each of the quarterback's 10 professional seasons, including four in the AAFC and six in the NFL. But it's hard to argue with him. In those 10 years, Graham took his teams to 10 league championship games. And he won seven of them.

Brown was coaching at Ohio State University when he first got a look at Graham playing for fellow Big 10 team Northwestern University. When Brown got the chance to sign Graham for the new Cleveland Browns franchise in 1946, he did. Graham went on to lead the Browns to the AAFC title all four years of that league's existence. When Cleveland joined the NFL in 1950, the Browns won the league title that year, too.

In 10 pro seasons, Graham passed for 23,584 yards and 174 touchdowns. He could run, too, when he had to. He ran for 44 touchdowns on only 405 career carries.

A tremendous all-around athlete, Graham even played pro basketball for the National Basketball League's Rochester Royals for one year in 1946. Naturally, the Royals won the league title.

Other Milestones of 1955

✔ The University of San Francisco won its first NCAA basketball title. The Dons capped a 28–1 season by beating defending-champion La Salle College 77–63 in the championship game in Kansas City on March 19. Big center Bill Russell dominated on offense and defense (see page 56).

Tony Trabert

✔ The Chicago White Sox blasted the Kansas City A's 29–6 on April 23. The visiting White Sox equaled the modern record for runs in a single baseball game.

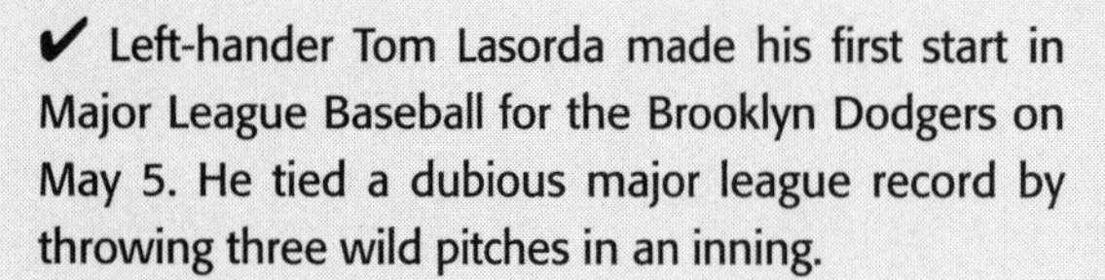

✔ Left-hander Tom Lasorda made his first start in Major League Baseball for the Brooklyn Dodgers on May 5. He tied a dubious major league record by throwing three wild pitches in an inning.

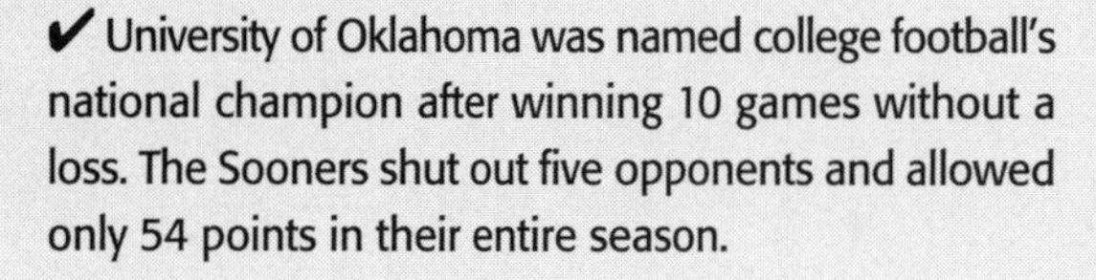

✔ University of Oklahoma was named college football's national champion after winning 10 games without a loss. The Sooners shut out five opponents and allowed only 54 points in their entire season.

✔ Tennis star Tony Trabert won the Wimbledon, French Open, and U.S. Open singles titles. Jimmy Connors matched Trabert's feat of three major titles in one year in 1974.

✔ Sudden-death overtime (where the first team that scores, wins) was used for the first time in an NFL preseason game on August 28. The Los Angeles Rams beat the New York Giants 23–17 after three minutes of extra time in the game (played, oddly, in Portland, Oregon). It was 19 more years before the NFL instituted overtime for regular-season games. Before that, games were simply recorded as ties.

✔ Sugar Ray Robinson was out of boxing for more than two years before returning to the ring in 1955. By December, the 35-year-old had earned a shot at the middleweight crown for the third time in his career. He won, knocking out Bobo Olson in the second round on December 9.

With runners on first and second base and nobody out in the Yankees' half of the sixth, catcher Yogi Berra hit a drive toward the leftfield corner. The left-handed Amoros, who had been positioned well off the foul line against the pull-hitting Berra, raced over and stuck out his gloved hand just before reaching the stands that ran along the foul line. He made the catch, braced himself against the stands, then whirled and threw perfectly to shortstop Pee Wee Reese (1918–1999). Reese picked runner Gil McDougald off first, and the Dodgers were out of trouble.

For all intents and purposes, that was the Series. The Yankees threatened again in the eighth, but Podres completed the shutout. For the first time, the Dodgers were World Series champions.

A Perfect 10 for Otto Graham and the Browns

"Otto Graham, you've just led the Browns to the NFL title. What are you going to do now?" In fact, Graham could have gone to Disneyland, because Walt Disney's vast amusement park opened in Anaheim, California, in 1955. Graham was even in the neighborhood after leading the Cleveland Browns to a 38–14 victory over the Los Angeles Rams in the NFL championship game on December 26 in Los Angeles.

Graham actually retired from football after leading the Browns to the NFL championship in 1954, and he meant it. But more than halfway into the preseason schedule in 1955—a six-game slate that featured five losses, including one to the College All-Stars—head coach Paul Brown knew it would be a long year if he didn't get his star quarterback back on the field for one more season. And, apparently, the 33-year-old Graham wasn't quite ready to put up his feet and relax, anyway. Brown made the phone call, and Graham "came back without too much coaxing," according to the coach.

Graham and the Browns started the regular season slowly, losing at home to the Washington Redskins before reeling off six consecutive victories. They finished the regular season 9–2–1 and qualified to meet the Rams for the NFL title.

The contest was a mismatch. Using a spread offense much of the game (a strategy that sent receivers to many parts of the field), Graham completed 14 of 25 passes for 209 yards and three touchdowns. He also ran for two touchdowns, and Cleveland's defense intercepted six passes from Rams quarterback Norm Van Brocklin.

After the game, Graham ran up the Los Angeles Coliseum tunnel to a standing ovation from a championship game record 85,693 fans. This time, his retirement was for good. He left a record of success unmatched in pro football history. In his 10 seasons with the Browns, including four in the defunct All-America Football Conference and six in the NFL, Graham took his teams to 10 league championship games.

The Colts Make a Good Call

Late in 1955, Baltimore Colts general manager Don Kellett was looking for a backup to starting quarterback George Shaw. So he made an 80-cent phone call to the Pittsburgh area to talk to a lanky 22-year-old named Johnny Unitas.

Unitas was a college star at University of Louisville, but was not taken until the ninth round of the 1955 NFL draft by the Pittsburgh Steelers. The Steelers decided not to sign him, and Unitas was paying his bills by operating a pile driver while playing for the Pittsburgh-area's semipro Bloomfield Rams for six dollars a game.

Kellett never could have imagined the return on his small investment. Unitas went to training camp in 1956 and made the team, then was pressed into service when Shaw was injured in the Colts' fourth game. Unitas never gave up the starting job, and went on to become one of the greatest quarterbacks in NFL history.

1956

Two Skating Golds in Winter Olympics

Only two Americans struck gold at the Winter Olympics in February in Cortina d'Ampezzo, Italy: Reigning world champions Hayes Jenkins and Tenley Albright won the men's and women's figure skating titles.

Internationally, the Soviet Union sent a team to the Winter Olympics for the first time and won more medals than any other country. The Soviets' performance included a surprising gold in ice hockey. After sweeping through pool play, they shut out the United States and Canada to secure the gold. The United States took the silver medal by beating Canada 4–1.

Skier Toni Sailer of Austria made the biggest headlines, though, by winning gold medals in the downhill, slalom, and giant slalom events. Sailer became the first skier to sweep all three Alpine events at the Winter Games.

Medal Leaders: Winter Olympics

	GOLD	SILVER	BRONZE	TOTAL
USSR	7	3	6	16
Austria	4	3	4	11
Sweden	2	4	4	10
Finland	3	3	1	7
USA	2	3	2	7

The Dons Repeat Themselves

With center Bill Russell (b.1934) dominating on both offense and defense, the San Francisco Dons swept to their second consecutive NCAA men's basketball title. The Dons overcame an early 15–4 deficit to beat University of Iowa 83–71 in the final game March 24 in Evanston, Illinois. Russell had 26 points and 27 rebounds.

San Francisco's win capped a 29–0 season and extended its record winning streak to 55 games. No other NCAA champion ever had gone undefeated. Not only were the Dons unbeaten, they also were pretty much unchallenged. Few teams stayed close during the regular season. And in the NCAA tournament, eighth-ranked UCLA, number-18 University of

Golden Performance *Figure skater Tenley Albright won a gold medal for the United States at the Winter Olympics.*

Utah, number-seven Southern Methodist University, and number-four Iowa all went down by at least 11 points.

Russell and guard K.C. Jones were in the NBA by the time the 1956–1957 season started. Without them, the Dons stretched their winning streak to 60 games in December. Then it was convincingly stopped by University of Illinois, 62–33.

Still, the Dons reached their third consecutive Final Four in 1957, finishing third.

Hoops Streaks

San Francisco's 60-game winning streak stood for nearly two decades, until coach John Wooden's dominant UCLA teams broke it in the 1970s. The longest NCAA Division I winning streaks:

SCHOOL	CONSECUTIVE WINS	STREAK BEGAN
UCLA	88	1971
Univ. of San Francisco	60	1955
UCLA	47	1966
Univ. of Nevada-Las Vegas	46	1990
Univ. of Texas	44	1913

Ken Venturi's Masters Heartbreak

Twenty-one-year-old Elvis Presley soared to the top of the pop music charts with "Heartbreak Hotel" in 1956. Twenty-four-year-old Ken Venturi (b.1931) had a different kind of heartbreak when he let a big lead slip away in the final round of the Masters golf tournament in Augusta, Georgia, in April.

Venturi, an amateur, had a four-stroke lead over Cary Middlecoff and an eight-stroke edge over Jack Burke heading into the last day of the tournament. But in a brutal final round in which only two players broke par, Venturi soared to an 80. That was still good enough to finish ahead of Middlecoff, who shot 77 but trailed overall. But Burke's 71 gave him the victory. It was the largest final-day comeback in Masters' history.

Ironically, Venturi's collapse gave him unique insight into the woes of golfer Greg Norman (b.1955), who blew a six-shot lead in the final round of the 1996 Masters. Venturi was the commentator on CBS television's national broadcast. "You were telling them exactly what I was thinking," Norman marveled to Venturi years later.

"It's because I've been there," Venturi said sympathetically. "I've lost 'em and I've won 'em."

Philadelphia's Hometown Hero

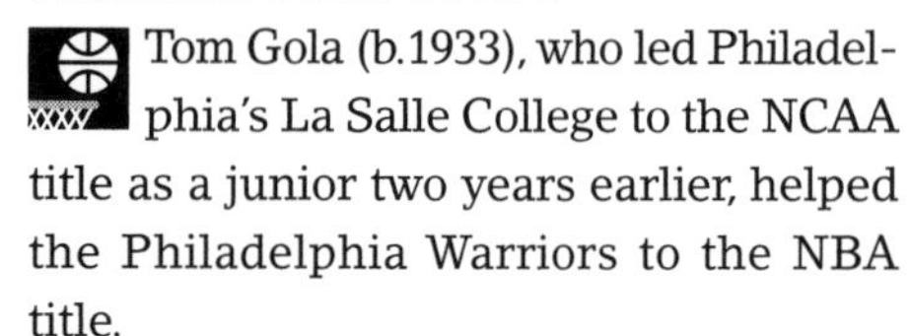

Tom Gola (b.1933), who led Philadelphia's La Salle College to the NCAA title as a junior two years earlier, helped the Philadelphia Warriors to the NBA title.

Gola was drafted by the team that included the league's top two scorers in 1955 (Neil Johnston and Paul Arizin), but finished last in the Eastern Division. At 6-foot-6, Gola played center in college, but moved to the backcourt with the Warriors. That posed particular problems for smaller defenders, and the Warriors turned their game completely around. "When Gola came, it changed the whole team," Philadelphia coach George Senesky said.

The Warriors went from last in the Eastern Division in 1955 (with a 33–39 record) to first in 1956 (with a 45–27 mark), then fought off the defending-champion Syracuse Nationals three games to two in the division finals. In the league finals against the Ft. Wayne Pistons, none of the first four games were decided by more than four points. But three of the decisions went to the Warriors, who then closed out the series with a 99–88 victory in game five at Philadelphia on April 7.

Long's Record Power Surge

On May 19, Pirates slugger Dale Long (1926–1991) hit a ninth-inning home run to help preserve Pittsburgh's 7–4 victory over the Chicago Cubs. It turned out to be more than a mere footnote, too. In fact, it was the beginning of one of the more sustained shows of power in Major League Baseball history.

The next day, the Pirates swept a doubleheader from the Atlanta Braves. Long homered in each game and drove in seven of Pittsburgh's 11 runs. Then Long hit the ball over the fence in back-to-back games against the St. Louis Cardinals and again in a doubleheader against the

World Series Gem *The Yankees' Don Larsen (without a hat) was escorted off the field after his perfect game.*

1956

Philadelphia Phillies. Finally, Long's blast off Brooklyn Dodger Carl Erskine on May 28 gave him home runs in a major-league record eight consecutive games.

Although Dodgers pitcher Don Newcombe stopped the streak the next day, Long's record still stands. Yankees first baseman Don Mattingly equaled the mark in 1987, but no one ever has homered in nine games in a row.

Don Larsen: Perfect Timing

Don Larsen was a rather ordinary pitcher who won only 81 games in his 14 major-league seasons. But he picked American sports' biggest stage in the 1950s—the World Series—to pitch the game of his life.

Larsen was 23 years old when the St. Louis Browns called him up from the minor leagues in 1953. He won seven games and lost 12 that year, then finished a dreadful 3–21 for Baltimore (the Browns had moved from St. Louis), which lost 100 games in 1954. But two of his three wins that year came against the Yankees, and New York acquired him in the off-season.

Larsen had the best years of his career with the Yankees, going 45–24 in five seasons. He was 11–5 with a 3.26 ERA in 1956, when he made 20 starts during the regular season. Against the Brooklyn Dodgers in the World Series, he couldn't hold a 6–0 lead and was knocked out in the second inning of Brooklyn's win in game two. But with the Series tied at two games apiece, Yankees manager Casey Stengel made Larsen the starting pitcher for the pivotal fifth game.

Larsen eventually pitched for the Athletics, White Sox, Giants, Astros, Orioles, and Cubs before retiring in 1967. He never approached the success of his Yankees years. But for that one afternoon in 1956, he was perfect.

Don Larsen's World Series Gem

Twenty-seven batters up. Twenty-seven batters down. No one on base for any reason in any inning. A perfect baseball game.

It's one of the most difficult feats in sports. Of tens and tens of thousands of baseball games played, only a handful of pitchers ever have thrown a perfect game. And only one did it in a World Series. That was New York Yankees right-hander Don Larsen (b.1929), who shut down the Brooklyn Dodgers in game five of the World Series at Yankee Stadium on October 8.

Few Dodgers even came close to getting a hit off Larsen. In the second inning, Jackie Robinson drilled a line drive off the glove of third baseman Andy Carey, but shortstop Gil McDougald grabbed the deflection and threw him out. In the fifth, centerfielder Mickey Mantle had to chase down Gil Hodges' (1924–1972) long drive in left center.

By the seventh, Larsen realized he was working on a no-hitter, but he was more concerned about winning the game. In the ninth, though, nerves got to him. "I was so weak in the knees out there I thought I was going to faint," he admitted afterward. But batters Carl Furillo (1922–1989) and Roy Campanella (1921–1993) went down easily, then Larsen struck out pinch-hitter Dale Mitchell. He had seven strikeouts and threw only 97 pitches in the entire game.

Larsen's gem gave the Yankees a three-games-to-two lead, and the rest of the Series was anticlimactic. The Dodgers eked out a 1–0 win in 10 innings the next day to force game seven, but the Yankees won the final easily. Yankee catcher Yogi Berra hit a pair of two-run home runs, and Johnny Kucks allowed only three singles in New York's 9–0 rout.

The Dodgers scored 24 runs in the first four games of the Series, with 13 of them coming in game two. Then their bats went silent. In 28 innings over the final three games of the Series, they managed only one run on seven hits. For the entire Series, they batted a meager .195.

Summer Olympics

By the mid-1950s, a new front had emerged in the Cold War between the United States and the Soviet Union. The two superpowers clearly had become rivals on the athletic field. In 1952, the Soviets sent a team to the Summer Olympics for the first time and fared well. In the 1956 Games in November and December in Melbourne, Australia, they flourished. (In Australia, summer comes during North America's winter.)

Medal Leaders: Summer Olympics

	GOLD	SILVER	BRONZE	TOTAL
USSR	37	29	32	98
USA	32	25	17	74
Australia	13	8	14	35
Hungary	9	10	7	26
Germany	6	13	7	26

The Soviet Union won more medals in Melbourne than any other country, including the United States. The Soviets were particularly strong in gymnastics, where they took nine of a possible 15 gold medals, including the men's and women's team titles.

The American team had its share of success, though, too. American men won 15 gold medals in track and field, including three by sprinter Bobby Morrow. Discus thrower Al Oerter (b.1936) won the first of his four consecutive Olympic golds, and the men's basketball team beat the Soviets for the title. In the swimming pool, the U.S. women swept the medals in the 100-meter butterfly and in platform diving.

Sooners Are Unstoppable

The University of Oklahoma Sooners began 1956 by running their record winning streak to 30 games with an impressive 20–6 victory over undefeated University of Maryland in the Orange Bowl on January 2. By the time the year ended, the Sooners' streak had reached 40 games after another dominating season in which they went 10–0 and won their second straight national title.

The Sooners steamrollered nearly every team in their path in the 1956 season. They outscored the University of North Carolina, Kansas State, and the University of Texas 147–0 to start the season, and went on to shut out six of their opponents in all. Oklahoma's average margin of victory: 41 points. Only the University of Colorado—the lone team with a winning record on the Sooners' 1956

1956

schedule—gave Oklahoma any trouble, falling 27–19.

At the other end of the college football spectrum, erstwhile powerhouse University of Notre Dame stumbled to a 2–8 record. That didn't matter to many Heisman Trophy voters, however. They awarded the trophy for best college football player to Notre Dame quarterback Paul Hornung (b.1935) in a close race over the University of Tennessee's Johnny Majors and Oklahoma's Tommy McDonald. It remains the only time the Heisman has gone to a player from a team with a losing record.

Floyd Patterson's Quick Rise to the Top

Floyd Patterson became boxing's heavyweight champion when he knocked out Archie Moore in the fifth round of their title bout in Chicago on November 30. The championship had been vacant since Rocky Marciano retired after knocking out Moore in September, 1955.

Patterson, the Olympic gold medalist in 1952, was only 21 when he won the title. He was the youngest heavyweight champion in history to the time (that distinction now

Other Milestones of 1956

✔ University of Kansas men's basketball coach Phog Allen retired after 48 seasons. His teams won 746 games, including the NCAA title in 1952.

✔ Mickey Mantle won baseball's unofficial Triple Crown in the American League by topping the league with a .353 batting average, 52 home runs, and 130 RBI.

✔ Needles, ridden by David Erb, won the Kentucky Derby and the Belmont Stakes in horse racing's Triple Crown, but finished second to Fabius in the Preakness.

✔ Althea Gibson became the first African American to win a major tennis tournament when she took the singles title at the French Open in May. She also was the first African American to win at Wimbledon, when she teamed with Britain's Angela Buxton to win the women's doubles title in June.

George Halas

✔ For the first time, NFL regular-season games were broadcast on television to selected markets across the nation by CBS.

✔ George Halas retired as coach of the Chicago Bears, concluding his third 10-year stint as coach. But Halas, who was also the club owner, was back for another 10-year stretch beginning in 1958.

✔ Forward Bob Pettit of the St. Louis Hawks led the NBA by averaging 25.7 points per game. In the 10-year history of the league, only dominant center George Mikan had averaged more in a season.

Ring Kings

Ezzard Charles was boxing's heavyweight champion at the outset of the 1950s, having earned the title by beating Jersey Joe Walcott in 1949. The succession of champions in the 1950s:

BOXER	WON TITLE
Jersey Joe Walcott	July 18, 1951 (knocked out Ezzard Charles)
Rocky Marciano	Sept. 23, 1952 (knocked out Jersey Joe Walcott)
Floyd Patterson	Nov. 30, 1956 (knocked out Archie Moore)
Ingemar Johansson	June 26, 1959 (knocked out Floyd Patterson)

belongs to Mike Tyson, who was 20 when he became the champ in 1986).

Later in his career, Patterson, who was not large but was lightning-quick, became the answer to another boxing trivia question: Who was the first heavyweight champion ever to regain his crown? Patterson lost the title when he was pummeled by Ingemar Johansson at Yankee Stadium in 1959, but won it back by beating Johansson in a rematch at New York's Polo Grounds in 1960.

The Giants Win the NFL Title

For the first time since the Cleveland Browns entered the NFL in 1950, the league title game did not include Cleveland as one of the participants. With stars such as Otto Graham, Dante Lavelli, and Dub Jones retired, the Browns stumbled to their first losing season in franchise history, going just 5–7. The New York Giants took advantage and won the NFL's Eastern Conference, then beat the Chicago Bears 47–7 in the championship game on December 30 in New York.

Versatile halfback Frank Gifford helped the Giants compile an 8–3–1 record during the regular season by finishing fifth in the league with 819 rushing yards and third with 51 receptions for 603 yards.

The real story for New York, however, was its defense. Under defensive coordinator Tom Landry, who had retired as a player to become a full-time coach, the Giants allowed points and yards only grudgingly.

Chicago won the Western Conference with a 9–2–1 record behind the NFL's most prolific offense. The Bears scored 363 points, an average of 30.3 per game.

The championship, then, was a classic case of the irresistible force (the Bears' offense) versus the immovable object (the Giants' defense). New York, however, quickly turned an intriguing matchup into a rout.

The game was played on a frozen field, which was reminiscent of New York's victory over Chicago in the 1934 title game. That day the Giants changed into sneakers for the second half and took advantage of the surer footing to come back and win. This time, both teams wore sneakers from the start, but New York scored after only four plays, and the outcome was never in doubt.

1957

Jackie Robinson Retires

Jackie Robinson, the man who broke Major League Baseball's color barrier a decade earlier, officially retired from baseball on January 5.

Robinson's decision voided a deal that the Brooklyn Dodgers and New York Giants had agreed upon three weeks earlier. Brooklyn had traded Robinson for pitcher Dick Littlefield and $35,000. Robinson retired rather than accept the trade to the Dodgers' fiercest rival, although some reports suggest he already had made up his mind to retire before the deal was made. The soon-to-be 38-year-old was coming off the two least productive seasons of his career.

In all, Robinson played 10 years in the major leagues, batting .311. He was a six-time All-Star and played in six World Series.

Robinson led the International League by batting .349 for the Montreal Royals, Brooklyn's top farm club, in 1946, then was promoted to the majors the next season. As an African-American in an all-white sport, Robinson made an immediate and lasting impact, of course. But he also made an immediate impact for the Dodgers on the field, earning National League rookie of the year honors after playing in 151 games, batting .297, and leading the league with 29 steals.

Robinson's best year came in 1949, when he was named the National League's most valuable player after finishing the season with a league-leading .342 batting average and 37 stolen bases. He also hit 16 home runs that year, drove in 124 runs, had 38 doubles and 12 triples, and scored 122 runs.

In 1962, in his first year of eligibility, Robinson was inducted into the Baseball Hall of Fame. In 1997, Major League Baseball celebrated the golden anniversary of Robinson's landmark season integrating baseball by officially retiring his uniform number, 42.

Tar Heels Put in Extra Work to Win a Title

The University of North Carolina faced a tall order when it played the University of Kansas in the championship game of the NCAA tournament March 23 in Kansas City. Not only were the North Carolina Tar Heels worn out from a three-

The NCAA's Unbeaten Teams

The NCAA didn't have an undefeated national basketball champion until San Francisco did it in 1956. Then North Carolina made it two in a row in 1957. The only unbeaten champs in history:

SCHOOL	RECORD	SEASON
San Francisco	29-0	1955–56
North Carolina	32-0	1956–57
UCLA	30-0	1963–64
UCLA	30-0	1966–67
UCLA	30-0	1971–72
UCLA	30-0	1972–73
Indiana	32-0	1975–76

overtime victory over Michigan State University the night before, they also had to face Wilt Chamberlain (1936–1999), the Kansas Jayhawks' dominating seven-foot sophomore center.

On top of that, the final game went another three overtimes. But North Carolina prevailed 54–53, preserving its unbeaten season and winning its first NCAA title.

The Tar Heels jumped to an early 19–2 lead, but Kansas clawed back within seven points at halftime, then overtook the nation's top-ranked team in the second half. The Jayhawks led 44–41 with two minutes left to go, before North Carolina rallied to tie the game at 46–46 and force the overtime. In the third extra period, Tar Heels center Joe Quiggs made

Celtic Pride *Bob Cousy (14) helped lead Boston to its first NBA title. The Celtics' dynasty, which produced 11 championships in 13 seasons, was just getting started (page 66).*

1957

two free throws with six seconds left to win the game and the title.

The Birth of a Dynasty in Boston

"The first one is always the hardest," Boston coach Red Auerbach (b.1917) said after his Celtics defeated the St. Louis Hawks in the decisive game of the NBA Finals. "It's also the most satisfying."

There's no question the Celtics' title came the hard way. They fought through a grueling seven games with the Hawks in April, including a double-overtime thriller in the final game. The issue was not decided until the Hawks' Bob Pettit's (b.1932) desperation try at a game-tying shot rolled off the rim as time ran out.

There's no question it was satisfying, too. For years, the Celtics had struggled to break into the NBA's upper echelon. They won their first playoff series in 1953, but did not make it to the finals until 1957.

Celtic Bob Cousy already was an established star, and when rookies Bill Russell, Tom Heinsohn, and K.C. Jones joined the team for the 1956–57 season, a dynasty was in the making.

Russell gave the high-scoring Celtics the one ingredient they lacked: an intimidating defensive presence in the middle. In 48 games as a rookie (he missed the first 16 games while helping the United States win a gold medal at the Olympics in Australia), he averaged a league-best 19.6 rebounds per game. He helped the Celtics post a 44–28 record, six games ahead of second-place Syracuse in the NBA's Eastern Division.

Meanwhile, St. Louis emerged from the Western Division despite winning only 34 of 72 regular-season games. The finals looked to be a mismatch. Instead, the series turned out to be one of the most taut in history—and one of the most important because it caught the public's attention.

The underdog Hawks stunned the Celtics by taking game one in Boston in double overtime by two points. St. Louis also won games three and six by two points each, forcing a seventh and deciding game at the Boston Garden.

Pettit sent the game into overtime with two free throws late in regulation, then Jack Coleman forced another overtime with a basket near the end of the first extra session. Finally, Boston hung on to

Kentucky Derby Winners

Iron Liege beat Gallant Man by a nose to win the Kentucky Derby on May 4. The list of winners at Churchill Downs in the 1950s:

YEAR	WINNER
1950	Middleground
1951	Count Turf
1952	Hill Gail
1953	Dark Star
1954	Determine
1955	Swaps
1956	Needles
1957	Iron Liege
1958	Tim Tam
1959	Tomy Lee

win 125–123 in double overtime behind Heinsohn's 37 points.

Little could Auerbach and the Celtics know the dynasty that the thrilling victory had spawned. Although Boston would lose to the Hawks in the finals the next year, its 1957 title was the first of 11 NBA championships in 13 years.

Unfinished Business

Bill Shoemaker was arguably the most successful jockey in the history of thoroughbred racing (see page 84), but he made an unlikely mistake on May 4 while riding Gallant Man in the Kentucky Derby.

Two years earlier, Shoemaker won the Kentucky Derby for the first time when he took Swaps to the Winner's Circle. In 1957, it looked like he would have his second winner in three years as he guided Gallant Man down the stretch ahead of the field.

Suddenly, Shoemaker stood up in the saddle—he had mistaken the 16th pole for the finish line (race tracks have striped poles at various spots around the oval to help jockeys gauge distances). Shoemaker quickly realized his mistake and tried to get his horse to the finish first, but it was too late. Iron Liege burst past Gallant Man to win the race.

Afterward, Shoemaker made no excuses. "I made a mistake," he said, though other riders argued that Churchill Downs had changed the finish line that year.

Still, the incident did not mar Shoemaker's glorious career. He eventually won 11 Triple Crown races, including the Belmont Stakes aboard Gallant Man.

Landmark Victories *U.S. tennis star Althea Gibson made history when she became the first African-American woman to win at Wimbledon and the U.S. Open.*

Althea Gibson's Milestone Win

Racial tensions were at an alarming high in September, fueled in part by the furor over Arkansas Governor Orval Faubus' refusal to desegregate Little Rock Central High School. The Supreme Court ruled, in the 1954 decision known as *Brown v. The Board of Education*

Althea Gibson: Tennis Trailblazer

Althea Gibson first attracted notice on the worldwide tennis scene because of her race. Then she quickly attracted more notice for her skill on the court.

Gibson grew up in a poor family in Harlem, but soon would make it to Forest Hills (both are neighborhoods in New York), the site of the prestigious United States Open. When she was a youngster, her family couldn't afford to buy her a tennis racket, but a city recreation department employee recognized her potential and got her started in the game. She quickly distinguished herself on the court by combining a powerful serve with tremendous athleticism. She proved she could compete with the best players in the world when, at age 23 in 1950, she broke the color barrier at Forest Hills: She became the first African American to play in the U.S. Open.

Gibson breezed to a 6–2, 6–2 victory over Barbara Knapp in her first match at the Open on MONTH XX, , then drew Louise Brough in the next round. Gibson gave the reigning Wimbledon champion all she could handle and was leading in the third and deciding set when a thunderstorm suspended play. The next day, Brough closed out a hard-fought 6–1, 3–6, 9–7 victory.

By 1951, Gibson broke into the ranks of the top 10 players in the United States. After that, it was a series of firsts. She was the first African-American player to win a major singles title at the French Open in 1956, the first to win at Wimbledon, the first to compete on the U.S. Wightman Cup team, and the first to win the U.S. Open singles title.

Including doubles, Gibson won 11 major titles in her career. After winning the U.S. Open a second time in 1958, she turned pro. But without a women's tour on which to compete, she was relegated to playing exhibition matches. For a time, she embarked on an entertainment career and even qualified for the women's professional golf tour.

Although Gibson never had a chance to shine on the women's pro tennis tour, she helped pave the way for other African-American players—such as Zina Garrison and Venus and Serena Williams.

of Topeka, Kansas, that public schools must be desegregated. But when the first nine African-American students at Little Rock Central arrived for classes on September 4, they were turned away by the Arkansas National Guard, which was acting on Faubus' orders. Three weeks later, the students began classes under the protection of Army troops sent by President Dwight D. Eisenhower.

About the same time, Althea Gibson was striking a blow for equal opportunity on the tennis courts. On September 8, Gibson became the first African American to win the U.S. Open singles title. The 30-year-old Gibson, who already had made history by winning at Wimbledon in June of 1956, breezed past 1947 champ Louise Brough 6–3, 6–2 in the final. She capped a run in the tournament in which she did not lose a single set.

Vice President Richard Nixon presented Gibson with the championship trophy. Gibson successfully defended her title in the 1958 Open.

Double Trouble

From the strange-but-true department comes this baseball incident: Philadelphia Phillies star Richie Ashburn fouled off two consecutive pitches that hit the same woman in the stands during an at-bat on August 17.

Alice Roth, the wife of *Philadelphia Bulletin* sports editor Earl Roth, took her grandsons to see the Phillies play the New York Giants at Shibe Park. Ashburn's line drive into the box seats behind third base struck Roth, breaking her nose.

After a short delay in which officials tended to the injured Roth, play resumed . . . and Ashburn fouled off a pitch that struck Roth as she was being carted off on a stretcher.

Happy Camper *World Series hero Lew Burdette beams between teammates Red Schoendienst and Hank Aaron following the pitcher's Game 7 victory that gave Miwaukee the championship.*

Lew Burdette's Classic Series

Lew Burdette's (b.1926) pitching helped lift the Milwaukee Braves past the defending-champion New York Yankees in seven games in the 1957 World Series in October.

Burdette pitched all nine innings to beat the Yankees 4–2 and even the Series in game two, then pitched a seven-hit shutout in Milwaukee to win game five 10 and give the Braves a three-games-to-two lead.

After the Yankees took game six in New York, Braves' ace Warren Spahn (b.1921), who was in line to pitch game seven, came down with the flu. Burdette took the mound in Yankee Stadium on only two days' rest.

Milwaukee scored four runs in the top of the third inning, and that was more than enough. The final was 5–0, and again Burdette allowed only seven hits. He was noticeably tired at the end, but in those days most pitchers worked all nine innings of a game. Third baseman Eddie Mathews (1931–2001) preserved Burdette's second shutout in three days by snaring Bill Skowron's bases-loaded ground ball and stepping on the bag for a Series-ending force out.

Including the final six innings of his first start, Burdette shut out the powerful Yankees for 24 consecutive innings. In all, he was 3–0 in the Series with an ERA of 0.67. He struck out 13 and allowed only 25 base runners in 27 innings of work.

Burdette's performance capped a sterling season in which he compiled a 17–9 record and made the All-Star Game for the first time. It was just a hint of things to come, however. In 1958, he won 20 games for the first time in his career, and from 1958–1961, he compiled 78 vic-

Jim Brown: At the Top of His Game

Quarterback Len Dawson was the man the Cleveland Browns wanted in the 1957 NFL draft. But after losing a coin flip to break a tie that determined the order of selection, Cleveland found itself picking after the Pittsburgh Steelers in the first round—and the Steelers wanted Dawson, too.

The Steelers got their man (and Dawson turned out to be a Hall of Fame quarterback, though after playing mostly for the Kansas City Chiefs), forcing the Browns to "settle" for Syracuse running back Jim Brown. But they hardly settled. In fact, having Brown was an immense stroke of good fortune for the Browns. He turned out to be one of the greatest running backs—if not *the* greatest running back—in pro football history.

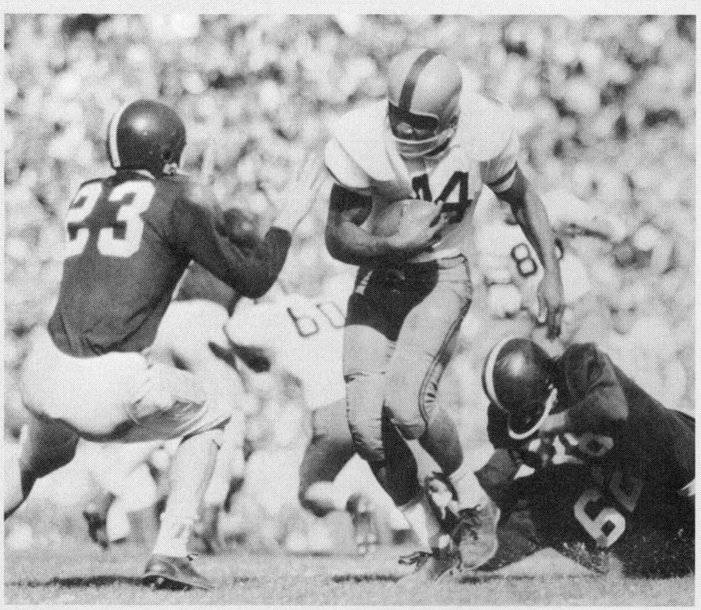

Jim Brown while at Syracuse University

Brown burst onto the scene in 1957, leading the league with 942 rushing yards (well ahead of runnerup Rick Casares of the Chicago Bears, who had 700 yards) and helping Cleveland return to the NFL Championship Game. He was named the NFL's most valuable player by the Associated Press.

It was an indication of things to come. Over his nine-season career, Brown combined size, speed, and power, plus a relentless competitiveness, as perhaps no other running back in the history of the NFL.

Brown's career statistics are staggering. By the time he retired following the 1965 season, Brown had amassed 12,312 rushing yards and 126 touchdowns, both NFL records at the time.

He ran for more than 1,000 yards seven times, led the league in rushing eight times, and played in the Pro Bowl nine times. He never missed a game in his career and ran for more than 100 yards in a game 58 times.

In 1963, Brown rushed for 1,863 yards (another NFL record at the time) and averaged an amazing 6.4 yards per carry. In 1965, he ran for 1,544 yards and scored a career-best 21 touchdowns. And then, at the peak of his career, he abruptly retired. While on location in London filming the motion picture *The Dirty Dozen*, Brown informed the Browns that he would not be back for the 1966 season.

Brown went out just as he came in: on top.

tories. Burdette retired in 1967 with 203 career wins in 18 big-league seasons.

Irish Eyes Are Smiling

The University of Oklahoma Sooners' record 47-game winning streak in college football came to a surprising end when University of Notre Dame went to Norman, Oklahoma, on November 16 and upended the top-ranked Sooners 7–0.

The Notre Dame Fighting Irish were a respectable 4–2 entering the game, but were coming off back-to-back losses to Navy and Michigan State in which they scored a combined 12 points. Oklahoma, meanwhile, had outscored its first seven victims by a combined 200–48.

The Irish shut down the Sooners' high-powered offense, though, and the game was scoreless heading into the fourth quarter. That's when Notre Dame put together the game's most impressive drive, moving the ball 80 yards and taking the lead on John Lynch's three-yard touchdown run. The winning run came on fourth down.

Those were the only points the Irish needed. Their defense limited Oklahoma to only 145 total yards. The closest the Sooners came to scoring was after marching to Notre Dame's 13-yard line in the first quarter, but they turned over the ball on downs. Oklahoma had scored in 123 consecutive games, another record.

Lions Roar Back to Beat the 49ers

The Detroit Lions and the San Francisco 49ers ended the regular season tied atop the NFL's Western Conference standings with identical 8–4 records, forcing a playoff at San Francisco's Kezar Stadium on December 22.

At halftime, San Francisco led 24–7, and the Lions could hear the 49ers' players whooping it up through the thin walls of Kezar's locker rooms. Outside, the hometown fans were lining up to buy tickets for the next week's championship game against the Cleveland Browns. Mentally, the 49ers were also thinking ahead to the next game. "We were very conscious of having that game in our back pockets," 49ers wide receiver R.C. Owens admitted years later.

That notion was reinforced when Hugh McElhenny (b.1928) ran 71 yards on the first play of the second half. But the Lions' defense held, forcing San Francisco to settle for a field goal and a 27–7 advantage. Then Detroit's offense exploded for three touchdowns in a span of just four minutes and 29 seconds to take a 28–27 lead.

Backup running back Tom Tracy was the star. He ran one yard for a touchdown, then raced 58 yards for another touchdown after a San Francisco punt. Gene Gedman's two-yard touchdown run in the first minute of fourth quarter put the Lions ahead for the first time in the game. The 49ers had four possessions after that and turned the football over each time.

The Lions won 31–27. It would stand as the NFL's greatest postseason comeback for 35 years, until the Buffalo Bills rallied from a 35–3 deficit to beat the Houston Oilers 41–38 in an AFC playoff game in 1992.

1957

Detroit Wins by Rote

The Cleveland Browns' absence from the NFL title game was short-lived. After a losing season in 1956, the Browns were back playing for the league title in 1957. They were routed by the Detroit Lions, though, 59–14 in Detroit on December 29. It was the third time in six years that Detroit beat Cleveland in the title game.

Other Milestones of 1957

✔ The Montreal Canadiens needed only five games to beat the Boston Bruins in the Stanley Cup finals in April. Montreal won its second consecutive NHL title.

✔ The University of California's Don Bowden became the first American to break four minutes in the mile. Bowden ran a 3:58.7 in a meet in Stockton, California, on June 1. At the time, it was the third-fastest mile ever run.

✔ Golfer Jackie Pung appeared to have won the U.S. Women's Open at Winged Foot. But Betsy Rawls was declared the winner after Pung signed an incorrect scorecard.

✔ Floyd Patterson successfully defended his heavyweight boxing title at New York's Polo Grounds on July 29. Patterson knocked out challenger Tommy Jackson in the 10th round. A month later, Patterson beat Pete Rademache in Seattle.

✔ Pete Rozelle was named the general manager of the NFL's Los Angeles Rams. Rozelle eventually became NFL Commissioner in 1960 and oversaw the league's most explosive growth period.

✔ The Little League World Series crowned a champion from outside the United States for the first time, when Monterrey, Mexico, beat La Mesa, California, 4–0 on August 23. Monterrey 12-year-old Angel Macias, who struck out 11, was the first player to pitch a perfect game in the final.

The Sod Squad: from the Polo Grounds to Candlestick Park

✔ Carmen Basilio won a split decision from Sugar Ray Robinson at Yankee Stadium on September 23 to capture the world middleweight boxing title.

✔ On September 24, the Brooklyn Dodgers beat the Pittsburgh Pirates 2–0 in the last game ever played at Ebbets Field in Brooklyn. The Dodgers then moved to Los Angeles.

✔ Baseball's New York Giants, who moved to San Francisco in 1958, played their last game at the Polo Grounds on September 29, also against the Pittsburgh Pirates. The Pirates won 9–1.

✔ The Los Angeles Rams beat the San Francisco 49ers 37–24 on November 10 before 102,368 fans at the Los Angeles Memorial Coliseum, a record crowd for an NFL game.

The Browns had staggered to a 5–7 record in 1956 as Tommy O'Connell, Babe Parilli, and George Ratterman unsuccessfully tried to fill legendary Otto Graham's shoes at quarterback. But O'Connell settled into the position in 1957 and led the league in passing while helping Cleveland compile a 9–2–1 record.

Detroit, meanwhile, was sent reeling when head coach Raymond (Buddy) Parker abruptly resigned at a public banquet before the season and became the coach of the Pittsburgh Steelers. George Wilson took over as coach and guided the team to the championship game.

The title game against the Browns was no contest. Detroit built a 17–0 victory in the first quarter and cruised after that.

Lions quarterback Tobin Rote passed for four touchdowns to key the rout. The most important scoring pass came from field-goal formation in the second quarter, when Rote stood up from his holder spot and threw a 26-yard touchdown pass to Steve Junker. It made the score 24–7 in favor of Detroit, and Cleveland never got any closer after that.

Rote finished the game with 12 completions in 19 attempts for 280 yards. He also ran for 27 yards and a touchdown. Junker caught 5 passes for 109 yards, including 2 scores.

The Alley-Oop

The San Francisco 49ers popularized the "Alley-Oop" pass in 1957. When the 49ers got close enough to the goal line, wide receiver R.C. Owens staked out a place in the end zone and awaited a high lob pass from quarterback Y.A. Tittle (b.1926). Then the 6-foot-3 Owens out-jumped the smaller defensive backs for a touchdown catch.

The play won a game against the Los Angeles Rams the first time the 49ers used it. Trailing 20–16 late in the game, San Francisco drove to Los Angeles' 11-yard line. Tittle lobbed the Alley-Oop, Owens caught it, and the 49ers won 23–20. San Francisco used it again for a touchdown in the final seconds to beat the Detroit Lions 35–31 in a regular-season game later in the year.

The Alley-Oop was named for a popular comic strip, whose title character used to swing from the treetops.

1958

A Good Decision for Sugar Ray

On March 25 in Chicago, Sugar Ray Robinson (1921–1989) regained the middleweight boxing title he had lost to Carmen Basilio the previous fall. The 37-year-old Robinson won a split decision in which both fighters traded blows back and forth.

The previous September, Robinson believed he had Basilio beat, but a split decision then did not go his way. Although he made no excuses that night, he admitted afterward that heading into the 15th (and final) round, "I was sure I had it at that time. But that shows you can't ever tell."

This time, Robinson decided he'd take no chances, going for a knockout in the final round. He staggered the champ with a barrage of punches, although Basilio withstood the punishment and finished out the round. The judges' decision was split in Robinson's favor, and he won the middleweight crown for a record fifth time.

Robinson continued boxing until 1965, when he retired at 44 years old. In 201 career fights, he was never knocked out.

Sweet Revenge for Pettit and the Hawks

In 1957, Bob Pettit missed a potential game-tying shot as time ran out in the Boston Celtics' game-seven victory over the St. Louis Hawks in the NBA Finals. But in 1958, Pettit and the Hawks turned the tables on the Celtics, beating the defending champions in six games.

In the April finals, St. Louis earned a key win in game one by edging the Celtics

Sudden Victory *Alan Ameche's touchdown gave the Colts the NFL title (page 78).*

104–102 in the Boston Garden. The teams were tied after four games, before another two-point win in the Garden put the Hawks in position to close out the series at home.

Pettit was the star in the decisive game six in St. Louis on April 12. He scored 19 of the Hawks' final 21 points in a 110–109 victory, including a tip-in with 15 seconds left that put St. Louis ahead by three. He finished with a playoff-record tying 50 points. Only Boston's Bob Cousy, who needed four overtimes to do it in a 1953 game, also scored 50 in a postseason game.

St. Louis' victory in the finals made the Hawks the fifth different NBA champion in five years. But it was clear that Boston was emerging as a powerful force. Indeed, the Celtics' loss in the finals was

1958

Once Is Not Enough

The St. Louis Hawks' NBA title in 1958 was the team's only championship (they moved to Atlanta in 1968). Here are the NBA teams that have won the most championships:

Team	Titles
Boston Celtics	16
Los Angeles Lakers	14
Chicago Bulls	6
Golden State Warriors	3
Philadelphia 76ers	3

(Note: The Lakers won five titles while in Minneapolis, the Warriors won two titles while in Philadelphia, and the 76ers won one title while in Syracuse.)

only a small bump in their road to becoming the greatest dynasty in NBA history. They went on to win each of the next eight league titles. It was not until 1967 that a team other than Boston (the Philadelphia 76ers) won the crown.

A Major Confidence Boost for Palmer

Arnold Palmer (b.1929) eagled (two shots under par) the 13th hole in the final round and went on to win the Masters golf tournament at Augusta, Georgia, April 6. It was the first major championship of Palmer's career, and the first of his four Masters victories.

The victory also was a tremendous confidence booster for the 28-year-old. Winning the Masters "told me something that I needed to know about myself," Palmer wrote many years later in his autobiography, *A Golfer's Life*. "That with the right kind of focus and hard work and maybe a little bit of luck, I could be the best player in the game."

That's exactly what Palmer became. He went on to win eight major championships, was the leading money winner on the PGA tour four times, and was named the PGA player of the year twice. He also was the first player to earn $1 million in career prize money.

Incidentally, Palmer's eagle helped inspire writer Herbert Warren Wind to coin the term "Amen Corner" for the famous stretch of holes 11 through 13 at the Augusta golf course.

A New Frontier for Major League Baseball

The National Aeronautics and Space Administration (NASA) was established in 1958 in response to Soviet advances in space technology, such as the 1957 launch of the satellite Sputnik I. America was on the verge of exploring the final frontier.

For Major League Baseball, the final frontier was the West Coast, and the big leagues finally stretched all across the country when the Dodgers moved from Brooklyn to Los Angeles and the Giants moved from New York to San Francisco in 1958.

The Dodgers and Giants immediately resumed their long-time rivalry when they met at San Francisco's intimate Seals Stadium on opening day, April 15. The Giants won 8–0.

Three days later, the Dodgers played in the Los Angeles Coliseum for the first time, and a major-league record crowd of 78,672 watched the home team edge the Giants 6–5.

Seals Stadium and the Los Angeles Coliseum were being used temporarily, until Candlestick Park and Dodger Stadium were completed.

Silky Sullivan Can't Catch This Field

Silky Sullivan's running style finally caught up with him at this year's Kentucky Derby horse race on May 7. The legend of Silky Sullivan began with his victory in the Golden Gate Futurity several months earlier, on December 7, 1957.

That day, the two-year-old colt broke from the starting gate, then promptly fell way behind the rest of the field. At one point, he trailed the leader by 27 lengths. Then Silky Sullivan made a mad dash to the finish and won.

Silky Sullivan's incredible closing kick would become his trademark. As a three-year-old, he won a race by rallying from 30 lengths back. Published stories have him winning from as many as 50 lengths behind, though undoubtedly the legend has grown over time. In the 1958 Santa Anita Derby, Silky Sullivan fell behind a mere 19 lengths midway through the race, before winning by three and a half lengths, ridden by jockey Bill Shoemaker.

At Churchill Downs for the Kentucky Derby, Silky Sullivan was the crowd favorite, if not the betting favorite. Sure enough, when the gate opened, he quickly took his customary place at the back of the field. Eventually, he fell 32 lengths back. Then he began his usual charge. The crowd roared as he passed one horse—and that was it. In this field, Sullivan's kick was not enough. He finished in 12th place, 20 lengths behind the winner, Tim Tam.

Tim Tam, ridden by Ismael Valenzuela, went on to win the Preakness Stakes as well. But his Triple Crown hopes were spoiled when jockey Pete Anderson rode Cavan to the win in the Belmont Stakes.

Major Accomplishment *Golfer Arnold Palmer (left) won the Masters tournament in Augusta, receiving this plaque from golfing legend Bobby Jones (right) who founded the Masters in 1934.*

Two Out of Three Isn't Bad

For the first time since the 1920s, the decade passed without a horse winning the coveted Triple Crown. But five horses came close in the 1950s. All five won two legs of the Crown, but placed second in the race they did not win. Those five horses:

1950	Middleground	Won Kentucky Derby; 2nd in Preakness; won Belmont
1953	Native Dancer	2nd in Kentucky Derby; won Preakness; won Belmont
1955	Nashua	2nd in Kentucky Derby; won Preakness; won Belmont
1956	Needles	Won Kentucky Derby; 2nd in Preakness; won Belmont
1958	Tim Tam	Won Kentucky Derby; won Preakness; 2nd in Belmont

Same World Series, Different Ending

In October, the New York Yankees and Milwaukee Braves met in a rematch of the 1957 World Series. This time, New York prevailed in seven games when Milwaukee pitcher Lew Burdette failed to repeat his final-game magic of the previous year.

For the second year in a row, the teams took the Series to a seventh game. And for the second year in a row, Burdette came back on only two days' rest to try to nail down a title for the Braves. This time, though, he was coming off a rocky outing in game five, losing 7–0 when a victory would have given Milwaukee the Series.

Burdette had a little more success in game seven, limiting New York to two runs through the first seven innings, and the game was tied heading into the eighth. But Yankees slugger Bill Skowron (b.1930) blasted a three-run homer off Burdette and New York scored four times to win 6–2.

Yankees pitcher Bob Turley was a workhorse over the final three games. After giving up plenty of hits to the Braves in game two, he pitched a complete-game shutout in game five, got the final out in New York's extra-inning victory in game six, and pitched seven innings in relief to get the win in game seven.

Colts and Giants Play Pro Football's "Greatest Game"

The Baltimore Colts beat the New York Giants 23–17 in overtime at Yankee Stadium on December 28 to win the NFL championship. The thrilling climax to the 1958 pro football season has commonly come to be called "The Greatest Game Ever Played."

The truth is, from an artistic standpoint it was not a great game. There have been far better played games in the history of the NFL. But for sheer drama and lasting impact, the 1958 title game stands alone. "It may have been the best thing to ever happen to the NFL," said Colts defensive tackle Art Donovan (b.1925), one of many future Pro Football Hall of Famers on the field that day.

That's because nationally televised sports broadcasts still were relatively new in 1958. And with much of America transfixed by the spectacle of the tightly contested championship game, it generally is credited with putting the NFL into the national consciousness. Add to that the

Johnny Unitas: Mr. Cool

The 1958 NFL title game not only put professional football on the national map. It also made Johnny Unitas a household name. The Colts' quarterback passed for a relatively modest 2,007 yards, with a league-best 19 touchdowns, during the 1958 regular season. But it was his poise under the pressure of the championship game, and his precision while directing the two-minute drill at the end of regulation time and the winning drive in overtime that left a lasting impression. (The two-minute drill is when football teams speed up their play in an effort to score before time runs out.)

Johnny Unitas

A lasting impression was something Unitas did not leave on NFL scouts early on. He was only a ninth-round draft choice by the Pittsburgh Steelers out of the University of Louisville in 1955, and he soon was cut from the team. "Too dumb to remember the plays," one Pittsburgh assistant coach said.

So Unitas went to work running a pile driver and playing semipro football for $6 a game in the Pittsburgh area. The Colts found him there, and before the end of the 1956 season he was their starting quarterback, a position he held for most of the next 16 years.

After leading Baltimore to the NFL title in 1958, Unitas had one of his best seasons, statistically, the next year. He passed for 2,899 yards and a career-best 32 touchdowns. The Colts won the 1959 NFL title, too.

From 1956 to 1960, Unitas set an NFL record by throwing at least one touchdown pass in 47 consecutive games. Even in the current era, in which rules have been liberalized and passing is dominant, that record has never been challenged. Many football experts believe it will never be broken.

By the time he retired after one season with the San Diego Chargers in 1973, Unitas held nearly every NFL career passing record, including most attempts, completions, yards, and touchdown passes. Those records have since been broken, but the legend of Johnny U. will remain. He died at age 69 in 2002.

1958

drama of a fourth-quarter comeback and the first overtime game in league history, and there's a reason the game earned its lofty title as the greatest ever.

The Colts held a seemingly comfortable 14–3 lead and were driving in the third quarter before a goal-line defensive stand sparked New York. The Giants took possession of the football at their five-yard line and drove 95 yards to a touchdown, then scored again to take a 17–14 lead early in the fourth quarter.

It was still that way when Baltimore took possession at its 14-yard line with just 1:56 remaining in the game. Colts quarterback Johnny Unitas calmly threw an 11-yard pass to Lenny Moore. Then it was three straight passes to Raymond Berry for 25 yards, 15 yards, and 22 yards, leaving the Colts at New York's 13-yard line. Steve Myrha came on to kick a 20-yard field goal to tie the game at 17–17 with seven seconds left.

Regulation play ended that way, and many of the players did not know what came next. After all, no NFL title game had ever been tied after four quarters. Sudden-death overtime is what they learned came next: The first team to score, won the game and the title.

Ernie Banks: Let's Play Two!

At 72 wins and 82 losses, and 20 games out of first place, the Chicago Cubs had a typically forgettable season in 1958—forgettable, that is, except for the play of Ernie Banks.

Banks became the first shortstop in history to lead his league in home runs, when he belted 47. He also led the National League in runs batted in (129) and slugging percentage (.614) while hitting for a .313 average. Although Chicago finished tied for fifth place in the eight-team league, Banks was the runaway choice as the N.L.'s most valuable player for 1958, easily outdistancing second-place Willie Mays of the San Francisco Giants.

The first African-American player in Cubs' history, Banks never played in the minor leagues, going directly to Chicago from the Kansas City Monarchs of the Negro Leagues late in 1953. By 1954, he was the Cubs' full-time starting shortstop, and in 1955 he hit 44 home runs (including five grand slams) and drove in 117 runs. From 1955–1960, he hit more home runs (248) than any other player in the major leagues.

Banks proved his MVP season was no fluke when he was the choice again in 1959. He batted .304 that year while hitting 45 home runs and driving in 143 runs—though the Cubs again tied for fifth place.

In a 19-year career that ended in 1971, Banks hit 512 home runs. He moved to first base for most of the second half of his career, but his 293 home runs were the most at the time by a shortstop.

Still, for all of his prowess on the field, Banks was perhaps best known for his sunny disposition off it, no matter his team's struggles. The most popular player in Chicago history, he affectionately was known as "Mr. Cub." And he permanently endeared himself to baseball fans everywhere for his eternally optimistic proclamation, "What a great day for baseball—let's play two!"

Other Milestones of 1958

✔ Willie O'Ree broke hockey's color line in January, playing with the Boston Bruins. It wasn't until 15 years later that the second black, Mike Marson, entered the NHL.

✔ Three-time baseball MVP Roy Campanella suffered career-ending injuries in a car accident on January 28. The Los Angeles Dodgers' catcher was paralyzed when the car he was driving skidded into a telephone pole.

Roy Campanella

✔ Ted Williams signed a contract with the Boston Red Sox to play for $135,000. At the time, it made him the highest paid player in baseball history.

✔ Monterrey, Mexico, became the first team to win back-to-back championships at the Little League World Series in August. The following January, however, Monterrey was barred from the 1959 competition for using players outside its geographical area.

✔ The Montreal Canadiens made it a hat trick, winning their third consecutive Stanley Cup championship. They beat the Boston Bruins in six games in the NHL finals in April.

✔ Floyd Patterson defended his heavyweight boxing title successfully with a 13th-round technical knockout of challenger Roy Harris in Los Angeles on August 18.

✔ The University of Southern California's Alex Olmedo led the United States to an upset of host country Australia in tennis' Davis Cup final. Olmedo stunned Ashley Cooper, the world's top-ranked player, in the clinching match on December 31.

✔ The first national intercollegiate women's tennis championship was held. Players entered as individuals, rather than as a team; Darlene Hard of Pomona College won the singles title.

New York won the coin toss and took possession of the ball, but failed to make a first down and punted. Then it was Unitas' turn again. On third down and 15 yards to go from Baltimore's 36-yard line, he completed a 21-yard pass to Berry to move the ball into Giants territory. Alan Ameche ran 23 yards to the 20-yard line on the next play, and the Colts were in field-goal range. They never needed to try a kick, though. Four plays later, Ameche barreled in from the one-yard line for the winning touchdown run after 8:15 of overtime, and the Colts were the NFL champions.

1959

Lombardi Turns the Packers Around

Vince Lombardi (1913–1970) was hired as the head coach of the Green Bay Packers on January 28. Although Lombardi had no previous NFL head-coaching experience, he was the respected offensive coordinator for the Eastern Conference-champion New York Giants in 1958.

"Gentlemen, I've never been associated with a losing team," Lombardi told the Packers' players in his first team meeting. "I do not intend to start now."

Those were bold words, considering that Green Bay was just 1–10–1 in 1958. But Lombardi remained true to his intentions, and hiring him turned out to be a shrewd move by the Packers. Green Bay immediately improved to 7–5 under its new coach in 1959. By 1960, the Packers were in the NFL title game. They went on to win five league championships under Lombardi's direction in the 1960s.

And, no, Lombardi never coached a losing team. In 1969, one year before his death from cancer, he led the Washington Redskins to a 7–5–2 record. It was their first winning season since 1953.

Daytona Gets Off the Beach, Onto the Track

NASCAR founder Bill France (1909–1992) took stock cars off the beach, where they had been racing for years, and onto the newly built Daytona International Speedway in 1959. On February 22, the Daytona 500 was born. The race made its debut with a fantastic finish that kept fans on edge for three days—that's how long it took to sort out the winner.

Lee Petty and Johnny Beauchamp raced bumper-to-bumper over the final several laps of the 500-mile race, then sprinted side-by-side the down the stretch to the checkered flag (the flag that signals the end of the race). The finish was literally too close to call. Joe Weatherly's

Photo Finish *Lee Petty (car 42) won the Daytona 500 in a thrilling finish.*

lapped car (it was one lap behind the leaders) also crossed the finish line at just about the same time as Petty and Beauchamp, obscuring the view of France and other officials.

France named Beauchamp the winner, but Petty howled. So France called the results unofficial until photographs and newsreel footage could be viewed to determine the actual winner.

It took more than 60 hours for film to come in from news organizations from all over the country and for officials to review it, but Petty wasn't worried.

"I'm sleeping good because I know I had him beat by about two feet," Petty said afterward.

As it turned out, he was right. NASCAR ruled that Petty had won by two feet. But the real winner was NASCAR. The memorable ending of the inaugural Daytona 500 had the new race well on its way to becoming the most prestigious event on the NASCAR circuit.

The Stars Go Out at the NCAAs

The unheralded University of California Golden Bears won the NCAA men's basketball tournament in March, and they did it the hard way, beating teams led by future NBA stars Oscar Robertson (b.1938) and Jerry West (b.1938).

1959

Coach Pete Newell (b. 1915), who had taken the University of San Francisco to the NIT championship a decade earlier, guided California to a 20–4 record during the regular season. But the Golden Bears were ranked just 11th in the nation and did not have the star power of the Universities of Cincinnati or West Virginia, whom they met in the Final Four in Louisville, Kentucky in March.

Robertson's fifth-ranked Cincinnati Bearcats entered the Final Four averaging 84 points per game, and Robertson was the nation's leading scorer at 32.6. But California's defense was the difference in a 64–58 victory in which Robertson scored only 19 points.

West Virginia's West scored 28 points for the number-10 Mountaineers in the final, but it wasn't enough. The Golden Bears built a 13-point, second-half lead and held on to win 71–70.

Great Eight for the Celtics

The Boston Celtics began the longest title streak in NBA history by winning the first of eight consecutive cham-

Bill Shoemaker: An Incredible Ride

Bill Shoemaker rode two horses to victory in the Triple Crown in 1959: "Shoe" was aboard Tomy Lee in the Kentucky Derby and Sword Dancer in the Belmont Stakes. That ran his number of Triple Crown winners to four.

He also won a record four national riding championships in the 1950s (something no other jockey had ever done), his first full decade of racing—but it turned out he was just warming up. Shoemaker continued to ride for 41 years and compiled a record unmatched in the history of horse racing.

Shoemaker's first ride was as a 17-year-old in northern California on March 17, 1949. His first winner came at Golden Gate Fields, south of San Francisco, the next month. Then he burst onto the national scene in the 1950s, when he was the dominant jockey in horse racing.

In 1953, Shoemaker rode an astounding 485 winners. It was a record that stood for 20 years. Two years later, he won his first Kentucky Derby, when Swaps edged Nashua (see page 51). It was Nashua's only loss, and a defeat that would deny him the Triple Crown.

From there, the numbers are staggering: 8,833 career wins on horses that earned an astounding $123 million in prize money. He won 11 Triple Crown races, including the Kentucky Derby four times. The last, when Shoemaker was 54 years old, came aboard 17–1 longshot Ferdinand in 1986.

He should have won the Kentucky Derby another time, with Gallant Man in 1957, but he stood up in the saddle too soon and blew the race (see page 67). Still, he came back to win the Belmont aboard Gallant Man the same year—the first of his four Belmont winners in 11 years.

Shoemaker rode until 1990. He began work as a trainer the day after his last competitive ride. And although he was paralyzed from the neck down in a traffic accident in 1991, he continued to work with horses until his retirement in 1997.

pionships. Head coach Red Auerbach's team brushed aside the Minneapolis Lakers in four games in the finals in April.

After two of the most thrilling NBA playoff series ever in 1957 and 1958, the Celtics and the St. Louis Hawks appeared on a collision course to meet for the third consecutive season in 1959. With guards Bill Sharman and Bob Cousy combining for 40 points per game, and center Bill Russell averaging 23 rebounds per game, Boston compiled a 52–30 record during the regular season and won the NBA's Eastern Division by 12 games over the New York Knicks. St. Louis had even less trouble winning the Western Division. Their 49–23 record was 16 games better than second-place Minneapolis.

But a funny thing happened to the Hawks on the way to the finals: They never got there. They were stunned by the Lakers in six games in the playoffs. Minneapolis was led by new superstar Elgin Baylor, who averaged 24.9 points per game during the regular season and became only the third rookie in league history to make the All-NBA team.

The Celtics nearly stumbled in the playoffs themselves, but they outlasted Syracuse—which had won only 35 games but had acquired star forward George Yardley late in the season—in seven games in the division finals.

The finals turned out to be no contest. The Celtics, who had won 18 games in a row against the Lakers, kept the string going. Not even the brilliant Baylor could make a difference.

Boston won the first game by only three points, but a 128–108 rout in the second game had the Celtics well on their way to the first four-game sweep in the history of the NBA Finals.

Almost Perfect *Harvey Haddix pitched a perfect game against the Milwaukee Braves for 12 innings, only to lose the game in the 13th.*

Unlucky 13th Foils Haddix's Perfect Night

For 12 innings on May 26, the Pittsburgh Pirates' Harvey Haddix pitched one of the most incredible games ever. Then in the 13th inning, he lost it all.

Haddix got out the host Milwaukee Braves in order for 12 consecutive innings. No one in Major League Baseball history ever had taken a perfect game to extra innings. The trouble was, Haddix's Pirates couldn't score off Braves starter Lew Burdette, either. Although Pittsburgh had its share of baserunners, collecting 12 hits over 13 innings, neither the Pirates nor the Braves had scored any runs.

1959

Finally, in the bottom of the 13th inning, the Braves got a man on base. Felix Mantilla reached first on a throwing error, ending Haddix's perfect game. After a sacrifice bunt and a walk, Joe Adcock (1927–1999) spoiled Haddix's bid for a no-hitter, a shutout, and a win with one swing of the bat. Adcock drove the ball over the fence for an apparent three-run home run.

Adcock's hit turned out to be just a double, because Hank Aaron (b.1934), the runner on first, left the basepaths before scoring. Adcock passed him and was called out. Officially, the final score was 1–0. Unofficially, Haddix threw the best game ever by a losing pitcher.

Winners at the Indy 500

Rodger Ward averaged 135.857 miles per hour—a record at the time—to win the Indianapolis 500 on May 30. Indy 500 winners in the 1950s:

YEAR	WINNER
1950	Johnnie Parsons
1951	Lee Wallard
1952	Troy Ruttman
1953	Bill Vukovich
1954	Bill Vukovich
1955	Bob Sweikert
1956	Pat Flaherty
1957	Sam Hanks
1958	Jimmy Bryan
1959	Rodger Ward

How Swede It Is

Brash young boxer Ingemar Johansson may have been the only one at Yankee Stadium on June 26 who wasn't surprised that the Swedish fighter took boxing's heavyweight title from Floyd Patterson (b.1935).

Johansson had a tremendous amount of confidence in his powerful right punch, which writers and promoters called the "Hammer of Thor" or "Ingo's Bingo." He knocked out contender Eddie Machen in the first round with that right to earn a shot at the title.

Still, the 26-year-old was a huge underdog against Patterson, the reigning champ. But he came out swinging and began knocking Patterson down again and again. In all, Patterson went down an astonishing seven times before the third round was finished. The champ got up each time, but the referee mercifully ended the fight with less than a minute to go in the third round. Johansson was the new heavyweight champion by a technical knockout.

Johansson, who won his 23rd consecutive bout without a loss, only fought six more times. Two of them were against Patterson, however, who regained his heavyweight crown with a victory in 1960. Patterson won again when the fighters met for the third, and final, time in 1961.

Big Steps for Little League

Little League Baseball was founded in 1939 by Williamsport, Pennsylvania, resident Carl Stotz as a small community league. By the end of the 1950s, it had grown to include more than 5,000 local leagues around the world.

In August 1959, the Little League World Series was played for the first time at its present site in Williamsport. Hamtramck, Michigan, won the championship by beating Auburn, California, 12–0 in the final.

Also in 1959, Dr. Creighton J. Hale, the director of research for Little League Baseball and later the organization's longtime president, developed the modern protective helmet.

Swede Stands Tall *Ingemar Johansson of Sweden stands over American heavyweight Floyd Patterson, after the Swede decked Patterson in the third round of their championship fight. Johansson defeated Patterson to capture the title.*

The AFL Makes Big Plans

Slow-motion replay made its debut on television sports in 1959, but it was full speed ahead for professional football, which overtook baseball as America's favorite sport in the coming decades.

The rapidly growing popularity of pro football led to the formation of a new league to compete against the NFL. Dallas millionaire Lamar Hunt (b.1932), after being rebuffed in his efforts to get an NFL franchise, met in Chicago with potential owners from Denver, Houston, Los Angeles, Minneapolis, and New York on August 14. Eight days later, they met again in Dallas and officially started the American Football League.

The AFL made plans to start play in 1960. Buffalo and Oakland joined the five other cities represented at the original meeting. Minneapolis withdrew in January 1960, and was awarded an NFL franchise the next day. Clearly, the rivalry had begun.

A League of Their Own

The owners at the inaugural meeting of the American Football League called themselves the "Foolish Club" because they were foolish enough to try to compete with the established NFL. The original members of the Foolish Club:

OWNER	CITY
Lamar Hunt	Dallas
Bob Howsam	Denver
K.S. (Bud) Adams	Houston
Barron Hilton	Los Angeles
Max Winter and Bill Boyer	Minneapolis
Harry Wismer	New York

Other Milestones of 1959

✔ The Boston Celtics beat the Minneapolis Lakers 173–139 at the Boston Garden on February 27 in what was then the highest-scoring game in NBA history.

✔ The Chicago White Sox scored 11 runs in the seventh inning of a 20–6 victory over the Kansas City A's on April 22. Remarkably, they did it with just one hit—A's pitchers walked 10 batters and hit another (when a batter is hit, he automatically goes to first base), and Kansas City's defense made three errors.

✔ The Montreal Canadiens continued to dominate the NHL. Their Stanley Cup championship in April was their fourth in a row—and the 12th in 16 years for Canadian teams.

Mickey Wright

✔ Rocky Colavito of the Cleveland Indians hit home runs in four consecutive at-bats in Baltimore on June 10. Colavito joined Lou Gehrig and Bobby Lowe as the only other players ever to homer in four straight trips to the plate. Through 2003, 14 players had four homers in a game, though not in a row.

✔ Golfer Mickey Wright won the U.S. Women's Open at the Churchill Valley Country Club in Pittsburgh on June 27. She was the first golfer to win consecutive Women's Open titles.

✔ Wright won the U.S. Open, but Betsy Rawls dominated much of the play during the rest of the LPGA's schedule. Rawls won 10 tournaments in the year.

Although that rivalry was at times bitter, the emergence of the AFL wound up bringing unexpected benefits to the NFL. The new league brought even more exposure to the professional game and set in motion a series of events that eventually led to a merger between the two leagues—and the birth of the Super Bowl.

Nicklaus Is a Teen Golf Sensation

Ohio State University junior Jack Nicklaus (b.1940) became the second-youngest winner of the prestigious U.S. Amateur golf championship. He beat Charles Coe in the final round at the Broadmoor Country Club in Colorado Springs on September 19.

Coe, the defending champion, and Nicklaus, who did not turn 20 until January of 1960, entered the last hole of the 36-hole final tied. From off the fringe of the putting green, Coe's chip shot missed the hole by just inches. Nicklaus then made an eight-foot birdie putt to win the title. Nicklaus also won the 36-hole semifinal by one stroke over Gene Andrews.

The Dodgers Win out West

Once the Los Angeles Dodgers survived a three-team chase for baseball's National League pennant, winning the World Series was easy. In October, they drubbed the Chicago White Sox in six games to win a championship in only their second year on the West Coast.

Los Angeles, the Milwaukee Braves, and the San Francisco Giants battled during the season's final weeks. But the Giants faltered badly down the stretch, losing seven of eight games over the final nine days to finish three games out of first place. The Dodgers and Braves ended the regular schedule tied atop the N.L. standings, forcing a three-game playoff.

Los Angeles needed only two games to dispatch Milwaukee and head to the World Series. In the deciding game, the Dodgers scored three runs in the bottom of the ninth inning and one in the 12th to beat the Braves 6–5.

In the World Series, the White Sox rolled to an 11–0 victory in game one behind the pitching of Early Wynn, who pitched seven shutout innings, and the hitting of Ted Kluszewski, who blasted two home runs and drove in five runs. But the Dodgers came back to win the second game, 4–3, and even the series.

In Los Angeles, huge crowds flocked to the Memorial Coliseum, setting new records each day: 92,394 for game three, 92,650 for game four, and 92,706. They watched the home team win two of three games and take control of the series. In game four, Gil Hodges' solo home run lifted the Dodgers to a 5–4 victory and a three games to one lead.

Although the White Sox beat Sandy Koufax 1–0 in game five to send the series back to Chicago, Los Angeles quickly ended it. The Dodgers built an 8–0 lead in the fourth inning and won, 9–3.

It's Back-to-Back for Baltimore

In a rematch of the 1958 championship game at Yankee Stadium, the Baltimore Colts and New York Giants met in Baltimore's Memorial Stadium to decide the 1959 NFL champion on December 27. Much like the 1958 game, this one was also close through three quarters. But it quickly turned into a rout won by the Colts, 31–16.

Baltimore trailed 9–7 until stopping New York on fourth-and-inches in Colts' territory on the first play of the fourth quarter. After that, it was all Baltimore. First, quarterback Johnny Unitas capped the ensuing drive with a four-yard touchdown run to give the Colts the lead for good. Then, Baltimore's defense intercepted passes from Giants quarterback Charlie Conerly three times, one of which Johnny Sample returned 42 yards for a touchdown. The other interceptions set the stage for 10 more points, and by the time the barrage was over, the Colts led 31–9. "We came on like gangbusters and blew 'em out of there," Baltimore defensive tackle Art Donovan said.

RESOURCES

1950s Events and Personalities

American Decades: 1950–59
By Richard Layman (Detroit: International Thomson Publishing/Gale Research Inc. 1995)
Part of a century-spanning series, this book contains a chapter on sports events from this decade along with short biographies of key figures.

The 1950s
By David Halberstam (New York: Ballantine Books, 1993)
This book is written for an older audience, but it contains fascinating descriptions of the people, places, and events of the 1950s.

This Fabulous Century: 1950–1960
(New York: Time-Life Books, 1970)
This installment of the Time-Life series provides a backdrop of the people and events making news in this decade.

The Golden Age of Pro Football
By Mickey Herskowitz (Taylor Publishing, 1990)
A veteran sportswriter covers the period in NFL history during which it changed from a small-time, local sport into a national phenomenon.

American Sports History

The Complete Book of the Olympics
By David Wallechinsky (New York: Viking Penguin, 2000)
An extremely detailed look at every Winter and Summer Olympics from 1896 to the present, including complete lists of medal winners and short biographies of important American and international athletes.

The Encyclopedia of North American Sports History
Edited by Ralph Hickok (New York: Facts On File, 1992)
This title includes articles on the origins of all the major sports as well as capsule biographies of key figures.

Encyclopedia of Women and Sport in America
Edited by Carol Oglesby et al. (Phoenix: Oryx Press, 1998)
A large overview of not only key female personalities on and off the playing field, but a look at issues surrounding women and sports.

Encyclopedia of World Sport
Edited by David Levinson and Karen Christensen (New York: Oxford University Press, 1999)
This wide-ranging book contains short articles on an enormous variety of sports, personalities, events, and issues, most of which have some connection to American sports history. This is a great starting point for additional research.

ESPN SportsCentury
Edited by Michael McCambridge
(New York: Hyperion, 1999)
Created to commemorate the 20th century in sports, this book features essays by well-known sportswriters as well as commentary by popular ESPN broadcasters. Each decade's chapter features an in-depth story about the key event of that time period.

The Sporting News Chronicle of 20th Century Sports
By Ron Smith (New York: BDD/Mallard Press, 1992)
A good single-volume history of key sports events. They are presented as if written right after the event, thus giving the text a "you are there" feel.

Sports of the Times
By David Fischer and William Taafe. (New York: Times Books, 2003)
A unique format tracks the top sports events on each day of the calendar year. Find out the biggest event for every day from January 1 to December 31.

Total Baseball
Edited by John Thorn, Pete Palmer, and Michael Gershman. (New York: Total Sports, 2004, eighth edition)
The indispensable bible of baseball, it contains the career records of every Major Leaguer. Essays in the front of the book cover baseball history, team history, overviews of baseball in other countries, and articles about the role of women and minorities in the game.

Total Football
Edited by Bob Carroll, John Thorn, Craig Neft, and Michael Gershman
(New York: HarperCollins, 2000)
The complete and official record of every player who has played in the NFL. The huge book also contains essays on a wide variety of topics relating to pro football.

Sports History Web Sites

ESPN.com
www.sports.espn.go.com
The Web site run by the national cable sports channel contains numerous history sections within each sport. This one for baseball is the largest and includes constantly updated statistics on baseball.

Hickok Sports
www.hickoksports.com
Not the most beautiful site and devoid of pictures, but filled with a wealth of information on sports at all levels. It is run by Ralph Hickok, an experienced sportswriter, and is regularly updated with the latest winners.

Official League Web Sites
www.nfl.com
www.nba.com
www.mlb.com
www.nhl.com
Each of the major sports leagues has history sections on their official Web sites

Official Olympics Web Site
http://www.olympic.org/uk/games/index_uk.asp
Complete history of the Olympic Games, presented by the International Olympic Committee.

The Sporting News "Vault"
www.sportingnews.com/archives
More than 100 years old, The St. Louis-based Sporting News *is the nation's oldest sports weekly. In the history section of its Web site, it has gathered hundreds of articles on sports events, championships, stars, and more. It also includes audio clips of interviews with top names in sports from yesterday and today.*

INDEX